THE EYE OF FAITH

THE EYE OF FAITH

Discovering the Most Powerful Driving Force of Your Life

Ron L. McIntyre

Copyright © 2002 by
HORIZON PUBLISHERS & DISTRIBUTORS, INC.

All rights reserved.
Reproduction in whole or any part thereof, in any form
or by any media, without written permission is prohibited.

First Printing: August, 2002

International Standard Book Number:
0-88290-714-X

Horizon Publishers' Catalog and Order Number:
1249

Printed and distributed
in the United States of America by

Horizon Publishers
& Distributors, Incorporated

Mailing Address:
P.O. Box 490
Bountiful, Utah 84011-0490

Street Address:
50 South 500 West
Bountiful, Utah 84010

Local Phone: (801) 295-9451
Toll Free: 1 (866) 818-6277
FAX: (801) 295-0196

E-mail: horizonp@burgoyne.com
Internet: http://www.horizonpublishersbooks.com

CONTENTS

Dedication 9

Preface 11

1. Discovering Attributes of the Eye of Faith 13
    A Surprising Discovery 14
    Very Successful, . . . However . . . ? 15
    The Eye of Faith??? 16
    The Relationship of Belief to Faith 17
    "Believing Is Seeing" 18
    "Cast about Your Eyes" 19
    "Give a place . . . to Believe" 19
    Is the Eiffel Tower Real? 20
    "Blindness" of the Mind 20
    Cause, Effect and Eternal Laws 22

2. Awakening a Sleeping Eye of Faith 25
    Anatomy of Mortal Processing 26
    ⬤s Form on Every and all Thoughts 28
    ⬤s Form Automatically and Continually 29
    ⬤s Remain in "Perfect Remembrance" 29
    Many ⬤s Are Distorted or Destructive 30
    Mortal Processing in Motion 32
    Levels of Decision and Agency 36
    Involuntary-autonomic Level 36
    Voluntary-responsive Level 37
    Invisible Origination Level 37
    Ultimate Command Level 38
    We must Understand Ourselves 39
    Who You Really Are! 39

3. Illuminating and Focusing the Eye of Faith 43
Anatomy of Spiritual Processing 43
Spiritual Processing in Motion 46
The Desire Illuminant 48
The Precision Illuminant 49
The Calm yet Alert Illuminant 49
The Fully Realized Illuminant 50
The Life-like Size Illuminant 50
The Living Color Illuminant 51
The Proximity Illuminant 51
The Perspective Illuminant 51
The Ambiance Illuminant 51
The Motion Illuminant 51
The Clarity Illuminant 52
The Continuity Illuminant 52
The Sound Illuminant 52
The Expedient Illuminant 52
The Touch Illuminant 53
The Real Intent Illuminant 54
The Initiative Illuminant 55
The Emotion Illuminant 56
The Intensity Illuminant 57
Essential Foundation Images 60
1. ✺s of God as Our Living
   and Loving Heavenly Father 60
2. ✺s of Jesus Christ
   As Our Example, Advocate, Redeemer 61
3. ✺s of Yourself As a Literal Child of God 65
4. ✺s of "the Great Plan of Happiness" 66
Additional ✺s Are Limitless and Infinite 74
Focus upon ✺s Anytime, Anywhere 75

4. Correcting Impaired Vision of the Eye of Faith .. 77
"Devices of the Devil" 78
Happiness: the Most Distorted ● 79
Discouragement: a Common ● 79
Mortal Eyes and Reality 81

Powerful ☀s Engage an Idle Spirit 83
Uniqueness of our Personal ●s 84
Distorted ●s and Sinful Consequences 85
Reality of Light and Darkness 86
Removing Beams from Our Own Eyes 87
Marriage Failure and Family Disharmony 89
Eye of Faith Sees the Invisible
And Children Respond 93
Eye of Faith in the Darkest Hour 95
Worry, Anxiety, Fear . . . or Faith 99
". . . And the Glory Be Thine." 99
Eye of Faith Must "Be Single to . . ." 100
Eye of Faith and Missionarying 101
Eye of Faith and Counseling LDS 103
Seeing "Things as They Really Are" 108
Strengthening the Eye of Faith 109
Cerebral Hemispheric Difference 110
Cerebral Hemispheric Balance 110
Cerebral Hemispheric Harmony 111
Exercise the Right Hemisphere 111
Relax the Body and Calm the Mind 113

5. Acknowledging the Power of the Eye of Faith . . . 115
Eye of Faith In Every Realm of Endeavor 115
- The Spiritual Realm 115
- The Therapeutic Realm 115
- The Affectionate Realm 116
- The Triumphant Realm 116
- The Aesthetic Realm 116
- The Well-being Realm 116
- A Combination of Realms 116
Eye of Faith = Temporal and Spiritual Power 116
Eye of Faith and Intra-dependence 117
Eye of Faith and Inter-dependence 118
Eye of Faith In Three Temporal Examples 119
- Eye of Faith and Diving the Dive 119

- Eye of Faith In a Jalopy Convertible 121
- Eye of Faith and Grades In College 123

Eye of Faith and Uplifting Others 125
Eye of Faith and Our Convictions 126
Eye of Faith, Learning and Remembering 128
Eye of Faith and Personal Prayer 130
Eye of Faith in Speaking and Blessing 132
Eye of Faith and Divine Communication 133
Reality of Radiance: Radiance of Reality 135
Eye of Faith and the Light of Christ 136
Eye of Faith and the Power of the Holy Ghost 137
Eye of Faith and the Gift of the Holy Ghost 139
Eye of Faith and Infrastructures of Matter 140
Eye of Faith and Electromagnetic Energy 141
Eye of Faith: Attracting and Propelling Power 143
Eye of Faith and Our Personal Radiance 145
Eye of Faith Sees Radiant Reality 147
Eye of Faith Hope and Charity 151
Eye of Faith In Adversity and Trial 153
Eye of Faith: Seeing
   "Things As They Really Will Be" 155

Bibliography 159

Scripture Index 161

Index 163

About the Author 171

To my children
Wendy, Shanell, Joni and their husbands;
and to my grandchildren
Bryant, Travis, Derek, Kierstie, Chelsie,
Trevin, McKenna, Brandon and Dallin,
I affectionately dedicate this book;
knowing the older ones understand,
and eventually all will understand,
why:
*"I have no greater joy than to hear
that my children walk in truth."*
3 John 1:4

PREFACE

We are endowed with a divine attribute unknown to the world in general, recognized but wholly misperceived by the Christian world, and little understood by Latter-day Saints. The Eye of Faith unveils a precious and powerful relationship between one's divine spirit and one's mortal intellect—a relationship that opens multi-directional channels through which divine communication flows, disables adversarial influences, brings one closer unto Christ and generates vigorous, invariable and steadfast faith.

This book, *The Eye of Faith,* presents doctrinal evidence that divine communication to mortal beings is deliberately symbolic in order to elicit visual concepts in harmony with the visual-conceptual language of the mortal brain. The book also presents compelling evidence that the mind dwells in one's own divine spirit, not in the mortal brain, nor in the body.

In addition, it shows that choices of thought should originate not in the brain but in the commands of the spirit, to which the brain faithfully and righteously responds when, and only when, the commands are delivered in compliance with the laws upon which such commands are predicated; elevating the scope and power of the Eye of Faith to a pinnacle of supreme significance during our mortal lives.

Another essential message of the book is that when one's Eye of Faith is either closed or dimmed, blurred or out of focus, or even clear but distorted, the individual's spirit is allowed to shrink from its divinely endowed power of control, and the responsive but undiscerning mortal brain, at any given moment, immediately and dutifully responds to "the natural man." At this point, although the spirit continues to enliven the mortal body, it assumes a subordinate role in the initiation of thought and the control of agency, and becomes "acted upon" to the detriment of both the mortal body and the divine Spirit.

And yet another essential theme of this book, *The Eye of Faith,* is that, conversely, when the Eye of Faith is righteously awakened, brightly illuminated and sharply focused, according to the divine laws disclosed herein, one advances from a mortal state of mind to a divine point of view, progressing beyond mere belief and even a brightness of hope to unwavering faith: faith to attain any blessing that is expedient and of which Heavenly Father approves.

> *"Do you look forward with an eye of faith,
> and view this mortal body raised in immortality?"*
>
> (Alma 5:15)

1

DISCOVERING ATTRIBUTES OF THE EYE OF FAITH

A series of simple yet remarkable incidents initiated a lifetime of meticulous research into one of the most precious and powerful attributes with which we are endowed during our mortal lives: the Eye of Faith!

When my wife and I were first married, we were students at Brigham Young University and could afford only a very small apartment. To cheer it up, I brought home a pound of jellybeans and placed them in a bowl in our tiny living room.

A few days later we were sitting in the living room and I was near the bowl of jellybeans. She asked me to toss her a cherry one, so I looked into the bowl for a red one and tossed it to her. I was in the mood for a lime-flavored one, so I looked back into the bowl for a green one. I was somewhat surprised because, as I looked for a green one, the green ones seemed to be far more numerous than the other colors.

What startled me so much was the fact that I remembered thinking, just seconds before, that this particular assortment must have been out of balance in favor of cherry, because it appeared that way to me when I looked for a red one for her. I really didn't think anything of the overabundance of red until the green ones appeared the same way.

This inconsistency sparked my curiosity, so I looked away from the bowl and made the decision to look for a licorice flavored one. When I looked into the bowl for licorice, I really was astonished to see the black ones appear more prominent.

I called her over and asked her to think of a flavor. I then told her to look into the bowl with the flavor in mind. She experienced the same effect. We tried it over and over again. The color didn't matter. It worked with all the colors. The only thing that did matter was that a specific flavor or color be in mind before looking into the bowl.

A SURPRISING DISCOVERY

I was scheduled to speak in church the following Sunday and realized that the unusual effect of the jellybeans would help me explain my subject. I really didn't know if the effect was a result of the shapes as well as the colors, so we cut out fairly large jellybean-shaped ovals from colored paper and pasted the ovals onto a large poster board so that four different colors were equally represented in a scattered array.

During my talk, I explained that I had just learned some things at BYU about the high incidence of color-blindness in men, and I just wanted to know how many in the total congregation could see different colors. I then revealed the board from where it was concealed behind the pulpit, and asked them by a show of hands to let me know if they could tell, of all the colors on the board, there was more red than any other color.

I was intrigued to see more than half of the congregation raise their hands. I then moved the board out of sight and pretended to bring out another one. Of course, the board I presented the second time was the same board. They didn't know that, and I said: "On this second board, how many of you can tell that there is more green than any other color?"

This time I was truly astonished when, again, more than half the congregation raised their hands. I then repeated the process a third time, with a third color, and their response was the same.

They laughed, and there were expressions of disbelief on their faces when I explained that they were looking at the same board each time. In fact, many searched around the piano and organ after the meeting, looking for other boards, convinced I had shown them three different boards.

That experience, unscientific as it was, kindled an interest that took me far beyond the color phenomenon into advanced research into the complex relationships between human perception, mental conceptualization, and the capacity and willingness to anticipate and to envision or foresee a respective consequence or fulfillment. In an effort to help friends, students and associates, I developed a therapeutic procedure to solve problems, overcome phobias, strengthen relationships and defeat addictions. However, I felt something very important was missing.

VERY SUCCESSFUL, ... HOWEVER ... ?

Although I was astonished at the remarkable results, I proceeded consciously and somewhat reluctantly.

- I saw some who had spent thousands of dollars to stop smoking, with no results, quit cold turkey.
- I witnessed college students with failing grades in various subjects change at mid-term to earn and receive straight 'A's by the end of the semester.
- One single mother raising a large family simply became consistently punctual and organized after every previous attempt had failed.
- Others instantly overcame phobias ranging from fears of public speaking to flying in airplanes.
- Parent-teen relationships were improved.
- Some credited the therapy with saving their marriages.

However, after so much success, I remained perplexed as to why the human mind had such potential for advancement and yet could be, and often was, so easily thwarted and totally deceived in so many ways by so many influences. I struggled with this dilemma for some time.

I had witnessed priesthood power many times and experienced the results of faith. I knew there must be a connection between (1) that glorious power, (2) the divine influence of the Holy Ghost, (3) the purposes of mortal life, (4) our agency so valiantly defended in the courts on high, and (5) our inherent attributes with which we are endowed by a wise and loving Creator.

Realizing that something very important was missing, I continued to search the scriptures and to seek further inspiration. While I continued that search, I ceased to use the procedure, except in a few instances in which friends sought help for the purpose of behavioral modification.

THE EYE OF FAITH???

One evening I was reading in the Book of Mormon of a time when the Nephites had become very prosperous. However, pride was increasing and the saints were becoming contentious. Alma decided to turn the judgment seat over to Nephihah and devote his full attention to the ministry.

He first went to the land of Zarahemla, and there said:

> Do ye exercise faith in the redemption of him who created you? Do you look forward with an eye of faith, and view this mortal body raised in immortality? (Alma 5:16)

Although I had read it many times before, the phrase "eye of faith" followed by the word "view" struck me this time with enormous impact. Because of my previous research, I recognized that the principle of faith described by Alma was in some way connected to a process of envisioning.

Later in his beautiful discourse on faith, Alma emphasized the long-range scope of the Eye of Faith:

> If ye will not nourish the word, looking forward with an eye of faith to the fruit thereof, ye can never pluck of the fruit of the tree of life. (Alma 32:40)

Centuries later, Moroni recorded in his account of the Jaredites:

> And there were many whose faith was so exceeding strong, even before Christ came, who could not be kept from within the veil, but truly saw with their eyes the things which they *had* beheld with an eye of faith, and they were glad. (Ether 12:19)

I italicized "had" to emphasize that this marvelous blessing beyond the veil followed a previous opening of the Eye of Faith.

What is the Eye of Faith?

RELATIONSHIP OF BELIEF TO FAITH

In one form or another, "believe" appears almost 500 times in the Standard Works, and the Joseph Smith Translation reveals there were additional times the Lord said we must believe to receive. The following are only a few examples demonstrating that we must be in a believing state of mind to receive the blessing:

- "... believing that ye shall receive, then shalt thou receive ..." (Alma 22:16),
- "... believing that ye shall receive, behold, it shall be done unto you." (Moroni 7:26),
- "... believing, you shall receive ..." (D&C 14:8),
- "... believing that you shall receive, and you shall have ..." (D&C 18:18).

However, how do you believe something? You either do, or you don't. You cannot force belief. It must come naturally and genuinely. It does when you learn to open or awaken your Eye of Faith!

In many scriptural passages, the terms "belief" and "faith" are used interchangeably. The two terms are sometimes thought of as synonymous. However, there are important distinctions:

- *Belief* is, in a sense, passive, meaning agreement or acceptance only.

- *Faith,* on the other hand, is active, embracing reliance, confidence and trust sufficient to lead to works.

"One cannot have faith without belief, yet he may believe and still lack faith. Faith is vivified, vitalized, living belief."[1] Notice Elder Talmage's use of "vivified." Vivify means "to give life to; make come to life; animate." "Vivid" means "forming clear or striking mental images . . . bringing strikingly realistic or lifelike images to the mind."[2]

BELIEVING IS SEEING

President Boyd K. Packer said:

> There are two kinds of faith. One of them functions ordinarily in the life of every soul. It is the kind of faith born by experience; it gives us certainty that a new day will dawn, that spring will come, that growth will take place. It is the kind of faith that relates us with confidence to that which is scheduled to happen . . .
>
> There is another kind of faith, rare indeed. This is the kind of faith that causes things to happen. It is the kind of faith that is worthy and prepared and unyielding, and it calls forth things that otherwise would not be. It is the kind of faith that sometimes moves things. Few men possess it. It comes by gradual growth. It is a marvelous, even a transcendent, power, a power as real and as invisible as electricity.
>
> In a world filled with skepticism and doubt, the expression "seeing is believing" promotes the attitude, "You show me, and I will believe." We want all of the proof and all of the evidence first. It seems hard to take things on faith.
>
> When will we learn that in spiritual things it works the other way about—that believing is seeing?[3]

I would repeat that last phrase: *"believing* is *seeing!"*

---

[1] James E. Talmage, *Articles of Faith,* pp. 96-97.

[2] Noah Webster, *Webster's New World Dictionary of the American Language.*

[3] Boyd K. Packer, "What Is Faith?" in *Faith,* pp. 42-43.

CAST ABOUT YOUR EYES

After hearing Alma's discourse on faith, the Zoramites wished to know "in what manner they should begin to exercise their faith" (Alma 33:1). Alma referred to the prophets Zenos, Zenock and Moses to further demonstrate that we must plant the seed before we can ever hope to reap its blessings. In this particular case, the seed Alma is referring to is a belief in a future life and the divine mission of the Son of God. He said,

> Cast about your eyes and begin to believe in the Son of God, that he will come to redeem his people, and that he shall suffer and die to atone for their sins; and that he shall rise again from the dead, . . . that all men shall stand before him, to be judged at the last and judgment day, according to their works (Alma 33:22).

When Alma urged them to "cast about your eyes and believe," do you think he thought they would see those precious scenes with their natural eyes? Of course not. Alma's frame of reference continues to be the Eye of Faith.

GIVE A PLACE . . . TO BELIEVE

Let's examine in some detail Alma's wonderful discourse on faith to the Zoramites on the hill Onidah, as he invites us to "awake" and experiment upon his words:

> But behold, if ye will awake and arouse your faculties, even to an experiment upon my words, and exercise a particle of faith, yea, even if ye can no more than desire to believe, let this desire work in you, even until ye believe in a manner that ye can give place for a portion of my words. (Alma 32:27)

Here Alma accepts the fact that we may not be able to believe, so he suggests that if we "can no more than desire to believe," then he continues: ". . . let this desire work in you, even until ye believe in a manner that ye can give a place for a portion of my words."

How can we possibly "give a place" in our hearts or minds without conceptualizing it, or picturing it, in what Alma calls the Eye of Faith?

At this point, Alma compares the word, or the symbol of truth, to a seed, saying: "Now, we will compare the word unto a seed" (Alma 32:28). He does this because in his inspired wisdom he realizes that mortal beings do not think in words, but in pictures. He already understands what President Packer and others are telling us in our day. As the "word" likened to a "seed" enters our mind from either a written or spoken source, it elicits a visual image, an image that may be correct or incorrect, clear or hazy, accurate or distorted.

IS THE EIFFEL TOWER REAL?

During my mission to the French-speaking areas of Europe as a young Elder, I was privileged to view Paris from atop the Eiffel Tower. As I approached the tower, it became immense and appeared much larger than I had ever imagined it to be. Prior to seeing this famous man-made wonder, my conceptualization of it offered me *hope* and a *strong belief* that such a structure truly did exist.

But once I saw it with my own eyes I knew it was more than just a picture in a geography book. I *knew* it was real.

Since that time, my wife and I have had several opportunities to visit France. During her first visit to Paris, she could only hope and believe the Eiffel Tower really existed. My descriptions of it and pictures she had seen during her life enabled her have a fairly accurate concept of what to expect, so she fully expected to see it, although she was overwhelmed at its size.

I relate these experiences to make a very important point: we cannot believe in an event, in a circumstance, in a condition, nor in an object—even if it is as big as the Eiffel Tower—unless we can conceptualize it in some manner.

BLINDNESS OF THE MIND

Faith is the first principle of the Gospel of Jesus Christ (A of F 1:4), and it is everlastingly connected to the first and great commandment: "Thou shalt love (or serve or obey) the Lord thy God with all thy heart, might, mind and strength." (D&C 4:2; 59:5; 98:47; 2 Nephi 25:29; Mosiah 2:11; Alma 39:13; Moroni 10:32; Mark 12:30; Luke 10:27)

Were we to examine each of these four metaphors or levels of endeavor individually, we might say that:

Strength = *physical energy*—such as bodily power or force.

Might = *mental intensity*—such as will-power or determination.

Heart = *a condition*—such as hard, soft, loving, broken, contrite.

Mind = *a process*—such as thinking, choosing, planning.

There is a very significant relationship between the heart and the mind. Although at times in scripture "heart" is used in reference to thinking, it usually refers to feeling. It is a metaphor representing our capacity to be (1) *sensitive to,* (2) *receptive to,* and (3) *responsive to* divine influence. **Sensitive** meaning our ability to *perceive truth,* **receptive** meaning our ability to *receive truth,* **responsive** meaning our ability to *respond by applying truth.*

The "mind" in this formula, however, is a process of paramount significance, yet little understood. **In the mind dwells the power to choose what the others will be. It is the pivot point or central control that determines** the (1) *energy of the strength,* the (2) *intensity of the might* and the (3) *condition of the heart.*

Significantly, prophets in the Book of Mormon refer six times to "the blindness of their minds" . . . not hardness of their minds, but blindness . . . implying vision or seeing, or the lack thereof (See 1 Nephi 14:7; Jarom 1:3; Alma 13:4, 14:6; 3 Nephi 7:16; Ether 15:19).

Why?

CAUSE, EFFECT AND ETERNAL LAWS

Everything is cause and effect according to eternal laws. Everything is a result of something. Psychologists refer to this phenomenon as **stimulus and response.** Physicists refer to it as **action and reaction.** In the scriptures we read of the law of the harvest: ". . . whatsoever a man soweth, that shall he also reap" (Galatians 6:7).

Responses to stimuli, reactions to actions, results to faith, and all blessings are the result of the laws that govern them respectively:

> There is a law, irrevocably decreed in heaven before the foundations of this world, upon which all blessings are predicated—
> And when we obtain any blessing from God, it is by obedience to that law upon which it is predicated (D&C 130:20-21).

We may ask: why did Alma in at least one instance and perhaps others ask the saints to look into the future or "look forward with an eye of faith" (Alma 5:16)? He even said that unless they could see the future results with an eye of faith, they would never realize or have those results (Alma 32:40).

Why did Moroni tell of "many whose faith was so exceeding strong," because they looked into the future and "beheld with an eye of faith" to the extent that they "could not be kept from within the veil" and were permitted to see the results of their faith with their natural eyes? (Ether 12:19)

Why have prophets credited a lack of faith and the resulting disobedience to "the blindness of their minds," implying a form of vision, or the lack thereof? (1 Nephi 14:7; Jarom 3; Alma 13:4, 14:6; 3 Nephi 7:16; Ether 15:19).

Why did the Savior illicit images in the mind of important concepts with words such as "sheep," "salt," "mustard seed," "vineyard," etc.?

Why did Elder Packer refer to the popular saying "seeing is believing" and then ask: "when will we learn that in spiritual things it works the other way about—that believing is seeing?"[4]

Answers to these questions may be explained in an enlightening review of scriptures highlighting symbolism and visual representations in the Gospel. Elder Joseph Fielding McConkie reports:

> Symbols are the timeless and universal language in which God, in his wisdom, has chosen to teach his gospel and bear witness of his Son. They are the language of the scriptures, the language of revelation, the language of the Spirit, the language of faith.[5]

Ancient and modern scripture make it clear: To receive it, we must be able to believe it! To believe it, we must be able to "see" it! To "see" it, we must be able to awaken the Eye of Faith!

---

[4] Boyd K. Packer, *Faith*, pp. 42-43.
[5] Joseph Fielding McConkie, *Gospel Symbolism*, p. 1.

". . . awake and arouse your faculties . . ."
(Alma 32:27)

2

AWAKENING A SLEEPING EYE OF FAITH

As mortal beings, we are endowed with a divine attribute unknown to the world in general, recognized but still misperceived by the Christian world, and little understood by Latter-day Saints.

Modern revelation illumines ancient scripture and makes it clear that each person is an eternal intelligence with a divine and permanent spirit clothed temporarily in a mortal body. The key to awakening and the formula for focusing the Eye of Faith emanate from an understanding of the relationship between one's divine spirit and one's mortal brain.

There are specific reasons why Alma asked the saints to look into the future or "look forward with an eye of faith" (Alma 5:16), and later said that unless they could see the future results with an eye of faith, they would never realize or have those results (see Alma 32:40).

There are specific reasons why Moroni recorded that there were "many whose faith was so exceeding strong," because they looked into the future and "beheld with an eye of faith" that they "could not be kept from within the veil" and were permitted to see the results of their faith with their natural eyes (Ether 12:19).

There are specific reasons why Book of Mormon prophets credit a lack of faith to "the blindness of their minds," implying a lack of vision or seeing (1 Nephi 14:7; Jarom 1:3; Alma 13:4, 14:6; 3 Nephi 7:16; Ether 15:19).

There are specific reasons why Elder Packer referred to the popular saying "seeing is believing" and then asked: "when will we learn that in spiritual things it works the other way about—that believing is seeing?"[1]

These reasons are at the very heart of the Eye of Faith, and they become clear as we understand the relationship between our divine nature and our mortal intellect.

ANATOMY OF MORTAL PROCESSING

Some time after he was called to the Council of the Twelve, Elder Russell M. Nelson responded to the question, "What are your feelings about healing by faith?" with this thoughtful answer:

> All blessings are predicated upon law (see D&C 130:21). Faith is part of that law. The power of the priesthood is real, being the power by which worlds have been created and the dead restored to life. The interrelation of these forces may best be illustrated by relating an experience I had with President Kimball that he has given me permission to relate.
>
> About three weeks after I had implanted a pacemaker in President Kimball, his personal physician telephoned me to say that it was working only intermittently. We tried everything we could to make adjustments without another operation but to no avail. So President Kimball was readmitted to the hospital, and again I stood before him in my green operating clothes. After giving me his usual greeting of warmth and love, he asked me for a priesthood blessing. After that blessing was pronounced under the promptings of the Spirit, he replied, 'Now you may proceed to do the things that you must do in order to enable that blessing to be realized.
>
> We reoperated, found the flaw in the insulation of the electrical wire, and repaired it. Now the pacemaker functions as it

---

[1] Packer, *Faith*, pp. 42-43.

should. He knew and I knew that not even for God's prophet can exceptions be made to the eternal laws of the universe. Not even for God's Son could divine law be broken. Faith, priesthood power, and work necessary to comply with law were combined to bring the blessing the prophet needed at that critical hour.[2]

This is a stirring and beautiful example of the interactive relationship between knowledge of the mortal body and the power of faith. We are to learn as much truth as possible . . . and apply it. In the words of one prophet to another with advanced medical knowledge, skill and experience: "Now you may proceed to do the things that you must do in order to enable that blessing to be realized."

Thus we see: just as it is important for us to apply our knowledge of the heart, or any other vital organ of the body, to the extent at which we are capable, so should we learn about the brain, and apply thereof whatever we have been blessed to understand.

I have found the following illustrations to be helpful, even necessary, to simplify and clarify the intricate relationship between the divine spirit and the mortal brain, and thus between the nature of our behavior and the power of our faith. Although the illustrations may appear to be somewhat procedural, they are certainly not any more so than surgery. They are designed to help us understand why the incomparable Eye of Faith is so powerful, and how this divine attribute influences with such tremendous impact both the spiritual and temporal domains of our lives.

When we made the transition from pre-mortal life to this mortal existence, we entered a world in which everything was first a blur of images, uncertain sounds and physical sensations. As our eyes began to focus, sounds became more discernible and colorful objects caught our attention, especially if they were in motion, and images began to accumulate.

A few years later, we learned that little lines on paper are letters with names, and soon thereafter learned to connect the letters into

---

[2] Russell M. Nelson, from an address to Religious Educators, 13 Sept. 1985, published by the Church Educational System.

words that represent our images. As this happened to each of us, the perception of what is reality, or what may become reality, remains in the image. The words, whether spoken or written, only have meaning to the extent they illicit an image, and are useful only to the extent the image is accurate or true.

Through the years we have experienced a complexity of emotions, attended to increasing levels of information, and witnessed a diversity of events and circumstances . . . all of which are faithfully recorded in the form of images accompanied by relevant sounds, feelings and circumstances. *For the sake of simplification, they will be represented thus:* ⬤. They are the essence of our mortal lives and are forming continually in a life-long process.

Illustration 1

You may see them right now. For example, you may see a ⬤ of your mother, father, or brother or sister, or your vehicle, or your home, etc. In fact, you can see many ⬤s of each one. Anything you can imagine forms a ⬤. For a moment, think back to when you were in high school or some other time. Immediately you see ⬤s of those experiences.

⬤S FORM ON EVERY AND ALL THOUGHTS

A wise Creator withheld a portion of the mortal brain out of our direct control: the autonomic nervous system, maintaining the beating of the heart in the circulatory system and the breathing of the lungs in the respiratory system, etc.

However, that portion for which we will be accountable is wisely designed to automatically, immediately and continually form ⬤s with each and every mental conceptualization. A ⬤ forms from an original thought, a remembered event, a word spoken, heard or read, an emotion felt or a picture seen.

For example, when you hear the word "horse," you do not see the letterset 'h-o-r-s-e'. You do not see a word at all. You literally see a 🔵 of a horse. If someone says a "white" horse, suddenly the 🔵 is a white horse.

Of equal importance is to remember that the earthly body, with its mortal brain, does many things automatically that are contrary to the spirit. These are impulses over which we have control but to which we may yield.

The automatic and immediate formation of 🔵s by the mortal brain may be one reason the Lord was so direct when He said "Look unto me in every thought; doubt not, fear not" (D&C 6:38). Interestingly, worry and anxiety automatically occupy our thoughts when we assume to have little or no control over an event or its consequences.

🔵S FORM AUTOMATICALLY & CONTINUALLY

Not only does everything enter in the form of 🔵s, but they are coming in continually and they form automatically. In fact, we cannot stop them from forming.

For example, at the bottom of the following page are two words. Whatever you do, don't let them form a 🔵 in your mind. Are you ready? Remember, no 🔵s! Turn the page. What did you see? Of course you did. Everyone does. Once a 🔵 forms, it has the power to distort, reinforce, even impede or prevent the formation of corresponding 🔵s in the future. In reality, once perceived, our 🔵s actually affect everything we experience in life: how we view different personalities, how we view relationships, how we view right and wrong . . . everything.

🔵S REMAIN IN PERFECT REMEMBRANCE

Not only are 🔵s forming from all our thoughts, unavoidably, automatically and continually, but, most importantly, they will remain with us at least through the Millennium. For wise and divine purposes, to use the words of Alma, they will remain with us in a "perfect remembrance" (Alma 5:18). All of them will be present and observable, except those affected by repentance, at the final bar of judgment. Later, Alma said "our thoughts will also condemn us" (Alma 12:14).

Recognizing the longevity of our thoughts, President Spencer W. Kimball said,

> Men's deeds and thoughts must be recorded in heaven, ... it is not too great a stretch of the imagination in modern days to believe that our thoughts as well will be recorded by some means now known only to higher beings.[3]

MANY ⬤S ARE DISTORTED OR DESTRUCTIVE

Many of your ⬤s are good and helpful. However and unfortunately, many are exerting a distorted or detrimental influence on your life. For example, you are reading this in the English language because you speak and understand English. As a result, the words form fairly accurate ⬤s.

Illustration 2

However, if you were to see the word "pomme," or hear the word spoken, it would not create an accurate ⬤ in your mind, unless you already knew what this word means in French. It would create, rather, a meaningless, distorted, or even evil ⬤. Now, as you discover the word "pomme" simply means "apple," a more accurate ⬤ immediately forms in your mind—of an apple. If you knew "rouge" means "red" and you heard or read "pomme rouge," the apple in your ⬤ would appear red. *Distortions of truth or reality will be shown thus:* ⬤.

RED ROSE

---

[3] Spencer W. Kimball, *The Miracle of Forgiveness,* pp. 109, 111.

To further illustrate what happens, consider another French word, a cute word: "pamplemousse," pronounced pomp-la-moose. Were you to hear the word, would it create a ⊙ for you, or a ⊙? The last part of that word, "moose," may very well cause you to recall a previous ⊙ already in your experience. After all, you know what a moose is: a big deer like an elk . . . or, is it something made of chocolate?

So we see just how wrong or distorted a ⊙ may be, even when the distortion is innocent. The distortions above are not harmful, but notice how wrong you would be: a pamplemousse is not a big moose, nor is it a popular dessert. It is not a big animal at all, nor something very sweet. A pamplemousse is a grapefruit!

So you see, not only are our ⊙s forming automatically, and continually, but many of them are ⊙s. . . , distorted, counter-productive, harmful or evil. Some are the result of innocent distortions such as the "pomme" and "pamplemousse" examples above. Others are due to our physical limitations and our perceptual skills. Many, however, are far more damaging and are deliberately created by those who are "expert in the devices of the devil" (Alma 11:21) and result "In consequence of evils and designs which do and will exist in the hearts of conspiring men in the last days" (D&C 89:4).

The important thing to remember is that no matter how right or wrong, how true or false, how accurate or inaccurate they may be, they remain the ruling influence in our lives.

Think of the centuries of suffering, degradation and heart-ache because of the following ⊙s in the minds of the Lamanites:

> They were a wild, and ferocious, and a blood-thirsty people, believing in the tradition of their fathers, which is this—Believing that they were driven out of the land of Jerusalem because of the iniquities of their fathers, and that they were wronged in the wilderness by their brethren, and they were also wronged while crossing the sea. (Mosiah 10:12)

These powerful ⊙s were passed from generation to generation with destructive consequences.

MORTAL PROCESSING IN MOTION

The ◯s and ⬤s in Illustration 3 are greatly reduced in number and greatly increased in size to symbolize what actually takes place as we receive and interpret incoming stimuli, and as we organize what we express in the form of outgoing stimuli. They represent the myriad of mental transactions that determine everything we do through an electro-chemical network of neurons, dendrites and neurotransmitters sharing information via synaptic exchanges.

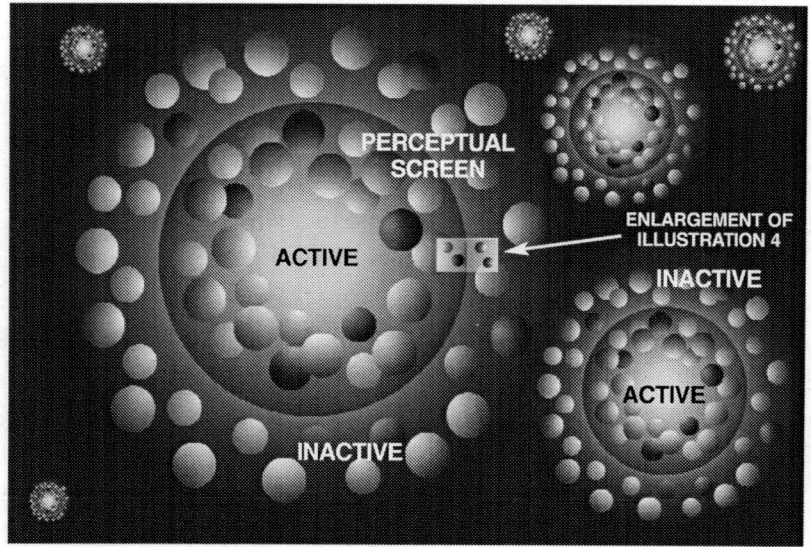

Illustration 3

Research reveals there is a naturally occurring barrier or perceptual filter or screen separating the total of all our ◯s and ⬤s into active and inactive domains by allowing into the active domain only those congruous or in agreement with those already in the active domain. Incongruous ones without corresponding ones in the active domain, regardless of how good or desirable they may be, are unable to enter. All others are relegated to the inactive domain where they exert no real or lasting impact upon our lives.

Although we may be able to recall them, they remain dormant or inconsequential. Conversely, a ⚫ regardless of how bad or undesirable it may be will immediately enter the active domain if a similar or corresponding one is already present.

The ⚪s and ⚫s accepted into the active domain comprise the ruling influences during our mortal lives. They control our perceptions of reality, our hopes and intentions, our personal values and beliefs, our misperceptions and deceptions and, as you will come to understand, the power of our faith.

In other words, only the ⚪s and ⚫s the active domain is prepared to receive will penetrate through the perceptual screen and enter the active domain.

This is why it is so important for us to read the scriptures, including the words of latter-day apostles and prophets; because those whose active domains are not prepared for eternal truths are among those "which have eyes to see, and see not; they have ears to hear, and hear not" (Ezekiel 12:2). These ⚫s or impediments may result from an intentional rebellious attitude because "ye have closed your eyes" (2 Nephi 27:5), or they may be due to innocent misperceptions, or they may occur because we are among those "who are blinded by the subtle craftiness of men" (D&C 123:12).

Literally thousands of stimuli of indescribable varieties are impinging upon our human sensory system throughout every conscious moment. To accommodate such a wide variety of incoming stimuli, there are actually numerous active and inactive systems throughout the brain in communication with one another.

Due to perceptual factors (explained in Chapter 4,) we are oblivious to most of the thousands of incoming stimuli to which our sensory system is exposed at any given moment. Of those we do perceive, many are distorted and inaccurate, even harmful and debilitating.

Illustration 4 is an enlargement taken from the rectangular section in Illustration 3 in which we see a ⚫ within the active domain.

Illustration 4

Because distorted, false, even evil ●s from society, etc. are in the active domain, other similar or corresponding ones are able to penetrate the perceptual screen and enter, allowing for even additional corresponding ones to enter in the future, as shown in Illustration 5.

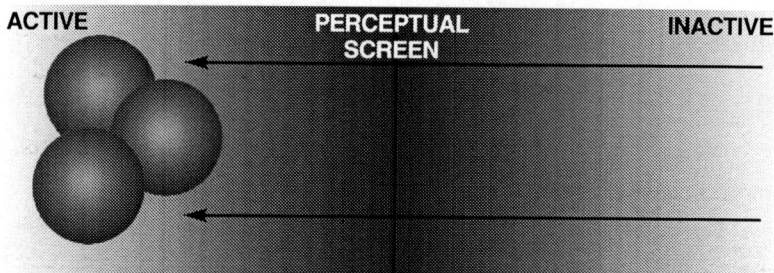

Illustration 5

Conversely, and all too often, in the absence of a corresponding positive, wholesome or righteous ●, an idea or principle we may want to believe, desirable as it my be, is rejected because the active domain has not been prepared to receive it, as shown in Illustration 6.

This is not a weakness, but rather a necessary condition for the fulfillment of our mortal probation.

For example, if a ● were present in the active domain that you are inferior, incapable or unattractive, even though you may be misjudging yourself, any and all new ones in agreement with the

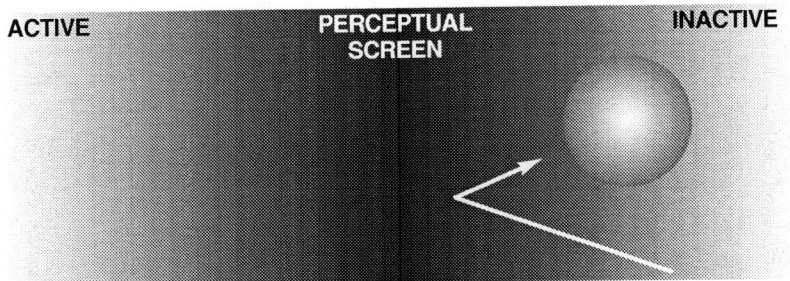

Illustration 6

existing one will immediately enter the active domain and reinforce the ◯ already in the active domain.

Furthermore, even if someone were to tell you that you are not inferior, not incapable, nor unattractive . . . even brilliant, this new ◯ will be rejected by the perceptual screen and relegated to the inactive domain because it is incongruous with the one already in the active domain. You may be able to recall the positive words spoken to you, but they will not change your self-concept nor modify the active domain until it is prepared to receive the new ◯.

Of even more significance is a distorted view of a righteous principle, an eternal truth: the nature of the true church, etc.

Unfortunately, our senses of sight, sound, etc. are unable to force a new ◯ into the active domain no matter how desirable it may be, unless it can penetrate through the perceptual screen. The key is, once again, the content of the active domain.

We not only filter or screen stimuli, but interpret or decode for meaning (see Chapter 4). Decoding is the conversion of incoming stimuli into meaningful conceptualizations. This is occurring continually and is a function of the relationship between our senses, the perceptual screen and the content of the active domain. Conversely, when we organize or formulate a message to speak or write or otherwise send, we convert or encode our conceptualization into stimuli we try to make meaningful to others.

The single term "receptors" will be used to refer to our human senses, such as sight, sound, touch, etc. by which we receive information or stimuli, and the single term "effectors" will be used to refer to the voice, actions, emotions, etc. by which we express or send information or stimuli.

The encoding system, like the decoding system, is flooded with stimuli, only a small portion of which can be transformed into vocal or observable behavior. For example, when you choose to say something, the final words you use, your tone of voice, the gestures you make and the look in your eyes represent in a highly condensed form only a fraction of all that you could have said and gestured, etc.

LEVELS OF DECISION AND AGENCY

Thus we see, what comes in, or what we decode via our receptors (see, hear, feel, etc.) and what goes out, or what we encode via our effectors, (say, write, do, etc.) is a result of the content of the active domain. How do we control the active domain? How do we determine its content? How do we overcome the processes controlling our mortal receptors and effectors, processes the Adversary well understands and employs to inject lies and distortions? How do we open the way for truth to enter, for noble ◯s to thrive, for hope to live, and for belief to flourish into unwavering faith?

To help us understand the significance of Alma's admonition to "look forward with an eye of faith" (Alma 5:16) and President Packer's penetrating question: "When will we learn that in spiritual things . . . believing is seeing?"[4] we must understand the differences and the relationships of our mortal nature to our divine spirit.

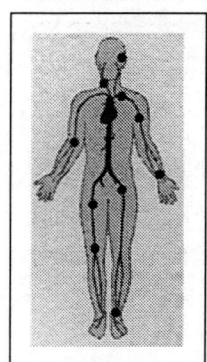
Illustration 7

INVOLUNTARY-AUTONOMIC LEVEL

At one level, the mortal brain performs involuntary functions without our conscious help, by operating our heartbeat and circulatory

---

[4] *Faith*, pp. 42-43.

system, our breathing and respiratory system, and our complex endocrine system, etc. The Autonomic Nervous System accomplishes these vital tasks through an elaborate balancing action between the Sympathetic and Parasympathetic Nervous Systems.

VOLUNTARY-RESPONSIVE LEVEL

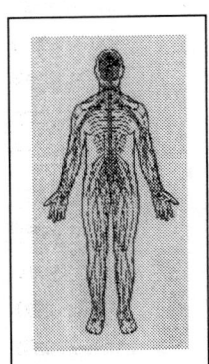
Illustration 8

At another level, the mortal brain performs voluntary functions in which motor neurons rouse our muscles into action when we choose to do something. The Somatic Nervous System makes this possible in a special relationship between the Central Nervous System composed of the brain and spinal cord and the Peripheral Nervous System which reaches out to the extremities of the body. Sensory neurons transmit messages *in from our receptors,* and motor neurons transmit messages *out to our effectors,* resulting in our daily behavior.

INVISIBLE ORIGINATION LEVEL

Illustration 9

At another level, neuroscientists are beginning to recognize a significant difference between the brain and what we may refer to as the mind. When we think of the brain, we often think of the mind. But the two are distinctly different. Medical and behavioral scientists are continually learning knew things about the brain. However, what we call the mind and the origination of thought continues to be a mystery.

Brain surgeons and neuroscientists have recognized that in addition to the brain, there is something invisible, something of a higher nature, wherein lies the ability to initiate a conceptualization, make a choice, and the capacity to use our agency to originate a thought at will.

ULTIMATE COMMAND LEVEL

Although the mind remains a mystery to modern science, for those who understand the plan of salvation, "it is clear that the mind of man rests in the eternal spirit," and that "man's intelligence is in his spirit and not in the natural or mortal body." Furthermore, "The mind was present with the pre-existent spirit; it will be present with the disembodied spirit in the sphere immediately following mortality."[5]

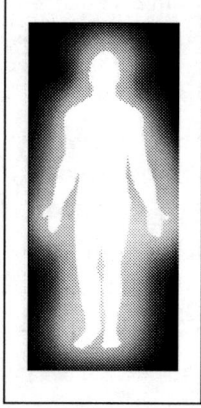

Illustration 10

The Prophet Joseph Smith spoke of "the mind or the intelligence which man possesses," and of using as synonymous terms, "the soul, the mind of man, the immortal spirit [i.e. the intelligence]."[6]

The marvelous invisible power to command your brain, therefore, dwells in your eternal spirit. It was with you in the pre-existence, it now controls your mortal brain, and it will continue with you after the death of your mortal brain and body.

In fact, we err when we assume that inspiration comes into our mortal brain. The Prophet Joseph Smith makes it very clear that inspiration and other forms of divine communication, "are revealed to our spirits precisely as though we had no bodies at all"[7] (See Chapter 3).

Furthermore, a significant word change was revealed to the Prophet Joseph Smith when he was translating Paul's oft-quoted definition of faith found in Hebrews 11:1. The King James Version reads: "Now faith is the substance of things hoped for, the evidence of things not seen." The word "substance" was changed to "assurance." Substance refers to something tangible, whereas assurance

---

[5] Bruce R. McConkie, *Mormon Doctrine,* p. 501.
[6] *Teachings of the Prophet Joseph Smith,* pp. 352-353.
[7] *Scriptural Teachings of the Prophet Joseph Smith,* p. 398.

is a mental state of mind, an inner conviction or point of view. Assurance comes from the Holy Ghost and is "revealed to our spirits precisely as though we had no bodies at all."[8]

WE MUST UNDERSTAND OURSELVES

Our need to understand the laws that govern ourselves was emphasized by President Brigham Young when he said: "The greatest lesson you can learn is to learn yourselves. When we learn ourselves, we learn our neighbors. When we know precisely how to deal with ourselves, we know how to deal with our neighbors. You have come here to learn this. You cannot learn it immediately, neither can all the philosophy of the age teach it to you: you have come here to get a practical experience and learn yourselves. You will then begin to learn more perfectly the things of God. No being can thoroughly learn himself, without understanding more or less of the things of God: neither can any being learn and understand the things of God, without learning himself: he must learn himself, or he never can learn God."[9]

WHO YOU REALLY ARE!

It is imperative that you always remember who you really are: an eternal intelligence with a divine and permanent spirit clothed only temporarily in a mortal body. **You are who you have been becoming since long before your birth, with the potential to advance further by learning to control a more tangible body and eventually return to the presence of heavenly parents.**

It is obvious that the mortal body responds obediently to the mortal brain, and that the brain responds to stimuli independent of or beyond itself. Although the source of this independent and invisible initiative is a mystery to science, modern revelation makes it clear that the marvelous power by which you control your

---

[8] *Teachings of the Prophet Joseph Smith*, p. 398.
[9] *Journal of Discourses*, vol. 8, pp. 334-35.

brain dwells in your eternal spirit: the real you. That power was with you during your pre-mortal life, and it will continue with you after the death of your mortal body.

Thoughts that control the body engage the Cerebral Cortex portion of the mortal brain. But where do they originate? Where should they originate? When they originate in the brain, we are like robots, with the brain controlling the brain. They should originate in your divine spirit wherein resides your agency and power of choice.

This is the agency our Savior defended in the courts on high, and which we supported in what we call the war in heaven during our pre-mortal lives.

For example, if I were to ask you to raise your right hand, your spirit could choose to do this, and your brain would then take over. The brain knows all the thousands of internal synapses and functions that must take place between the nervous system and the muscular system working with and against the skeletal system.

On the other hand, you could choose to raise your left hand instead of your right. Or, you could choose to do nothing at all, and your brain would obey. At what level do you decide whether you move or not, or how you move, or what you say, even what you think?

The point is this: the brain will do whatever it thinks it is supposed to do, right or wrong. The brain controls the movement, but you—the real you: your divine spirit—control the brain.

Although the spirit controls the brain and, in turn, the mortal body, it is important to realize that the mortal body may influence the spirit. In the words of Brigham Young: "Many think that the Devil has rule and power over both body and spirit. Now, I want to tell you that he does not hold any power over man, only so far as the body overcomes the spirit that is in a man, through yielding to the spirit of evil . . . The spirit is influenced by the body, and the body by the spirit."¹⁰

Once again we are reminded of the enormous and everlasting significance of the ⬤s and ⬤s in the active domain. Acknowledging their enormous influence, recognizing the dire need to control them, and realizing that the power to do so dwells in your divine spirit, helps you to awaken your Eye of Faith. This, however, is but the beginning. In the following chapter, you will come to understand that when your personal spirit illuminates and focuses your Eye of Faith, you will be able to bypass your mortal receptors such as sight, sound, etc., and the perceptual screens, to place your aspirations directly into the active domain. Otherwise, the body will all too often continue to respond to a mortal brain that continues to respond to the ⬤s of the natural man who "is an enemy to God" (Mosiah 3:19).

---

¹⁰ *Discourses of Brigham Young*, pp. 69-70.

"When a man works by faith he works by mental exertion instead of by physical force."
(Joseph Smith, *Lectures on Faith*, p. 61)

3

ILLUMINATING AND FOCUSING THE EYE OF FAITH

At the very heart of the Eye of Faith is the will to initiate and the capacity to engage your divine spirit in commanding communication with your mortal intellect in "the language of the scriptures, the language of revelation, the language of the Spirit, the language of faith."[1]

ANATOMY OF SPIRITUAL PROCESSING

Because the spirit is intended to be invisible to our mortal observation, magnetic resonance imaging (MRIs) and dissections of the brain reveal only electro-chemical networks of neurons, dendrites and neurotransmitters sharing information via synaptic exchanges.

However, permeating and giving life to that complex array of cerebral tissue, even at the atomic nucleus level, is our eternal spirit. As mortal beings, we are wisely endowed with a significant attribute that enables our spirit to communicate with, receive from and send to, our mortal brain. In fact, one of the reasons for which we are passing through this mortal realm is to learn to subordinate

---

1 Joseph Fielding McConkie, *Gospel Symbolism*, p. 1.

or subject "the natural man" to divine influence and overcome "the flesh;" to be in the world, but not of the world.

Our intelligences dwell in our spirit bodies, and our spirit bodies dwell in our mortal bodies. Our intelligences have always existed and they will always continue to exist. The Prophet Joseph Smith said: "The intelligence of spirits had no beginning, neither will it have an end."[2] Our spirit bodies were born of heavenly parents and are composed of a substance so refined and pure they are invisible to our mortal eyes (see D&C 131:7-8).

Although our intelligences reside within our spirits, we refer to this union as a single entity: our spirit bodies. Our spirit bodies dwell in, and give life to, our mortal bodies. However, the mortal body, with its mortal brain, and the spirit body are distinctly separate entities.

This distinction helps us to comprehend the monumentally significant relationship between the mortal brain and the divine spirit. The body responds obediently to the mortal brain, and the brain responds to stimuli independent of and beyond itself (see Chapter 2). Although the source of this independent and invisible initiative is a mystery to science, modern revelation makes it clear that the marvelous power by which you may command the brain dwells in your divine spirit, not in the brain nor any other part of the mortal body. In fact, inspiration and other forms of divine communication "are revealed to our spirits precisely as though we had no bodies at all."[3]

Significantly, the key to unwavering faith is the control of that vital relationship between the divine spirit and the mortal intellect. For the purpose of illustration only, the divine spirit is shown separated from the mortal body in Illustration 11.

However, in this life, just as the spirit is limited to the limitations of the body, so is it limited to the limitations of the brain. For example, if an arm is broken or amputated, or an eye is impaired

---

[2] *History of the Church,* Vol. 6, pp. 310-11.

[3] *Scriptural Teachings of the Prophet Joseph Smith,* p. 398.

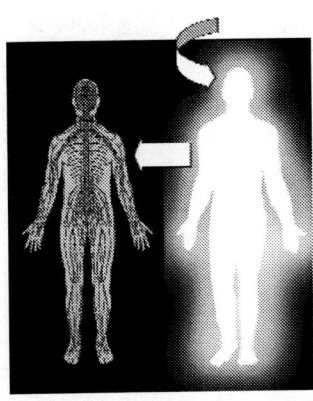

Illustration 11

or blind, the spirit is limited in mortal actions.

In a similar manner, the spirit is limited to inadequacies in our thought patterns. To help us to better understand the vital relationship between mortal thought and things of the spirit, the Prophet Joseph Smith said:

> . . . the things of God are of deep import; and time, experience, and careful and ponderous and solemn thoughts can only find them out. Thy mind, O man! if thou wilt lead a soul unto salvation. must stretch as high as the utmost heavens, and search into and contemplate the darkest abyss, and the broad expanse of eternity—thou must commune with God.[4]

In this powerful statement, challenging us to mentally "search into and contemplate . . . the broad expanse of eternity," and "stretch as high as the utmost heavens," the Prophet Joseph asserted the necessity of "ponderous . . . thoughts."

The Savior also taught the importance of pondering as an essential process in acquiring spiritual knowledge and understanding, in addition to prayer and beyond hearing and reading only:

> Therefore, go ye unto your homes, and ponder upon the things which I have said, and ask of the Father, in my name, that ye may understand, and prepare your minds for the morrow, and I come unto you again (3Nephi 17:3).

Consider this question carefully: can you really ponder something without at least a vague ◉ coming into view? Of course not. The correctness, truthfulness and righteousness of that ◉ is what gives meaning in spiritual awareness. It takes time and effort, but it is worth it.

---

[4] *History of the Church,* Vol. 3, p. 295.

Emphasizing the need to take time to ponder, President Ezra Taft Benson said,

> Man must take time to meditate, to sweep the cobwebs from his mind, so that he might get a more firm grip on the truth and spend less time chasing phantoms and dallying in projects of lesser worth. . . . Take time to meditate. Ponder the meaning of the work in which you are engaged."[5]

Thus we realize, ponderous mental effort, as emphasized above by the Savior, the Prophet Joseph and President Benson, opens communication externally between your divine spirit and the Holy Ghost, and internally between your divine spirit and your mortal intellect, opening pathways for insight, comprehension, promptings and confirmations.

SPIRITUAL PROCESSING IN MOTION

We now understand that just as the spirit is limited by physical inadequacies in the temporal or mortal body, the spirit is also limited by mental inadequacies in our patterns of thought. We must,

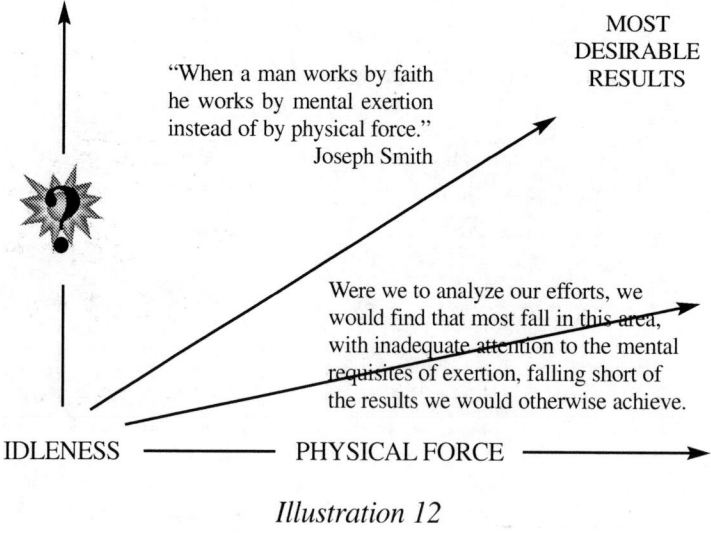

Illustration 12

---

[5] *The Teachings of Ezra Taft Benson*, p. 390.

therefore, learn to develop patterns of thought that embrace the admonition of the Prophet Joseph Smith: "When a man works by faith he works by mental exertion instead of by physical force."[6] Physical force may very well be a consequence of faith, but the initial point of faith is proper "mental exertion."

At this point, it is extremely important to realize that "Mental exertion" encompasses far more than mere wishful thinking. You may have wondered what the translucent image is behind the question mark in Illustration 12. Just as knowing how to breath does not make us lung or pulmonary specialists, merely knowing how to think does not engage the divine spirit in commanding communication with the mortal brain.

We must initiate the will and develop the capacity to engage our personal and divine spirits in commanding communication with our own mortal intellects in "the language of the scriptures, the language of revelation, the language of the Spirit, the language of faith."[7]

Focusing your Eye of Faith is a pleasant experience. However, this glorious process will require effort, mental effort . . . in the words of the Prophet Joseph: "mental exertion."[8]

The marvelous and inexpressible transaction between the spirit and the brain will be shown by this symbol, ✺ which represents that precious moment when we, in Alma's words, "look forward with an eye of faith, and view . . ." (Alma 5:16) the actual object of our faith, the hoped-for event, the anticipated condition, the literal expectation of the desirable result as did the righteous Jaredites "who could

Illustration 13

---

[6] *Lectures on Faith*, p. 61.

[7] McConkie, *Gospel Symbolism*, p. 1.

[8] Smith, *History of the Church*, p. 61.

not be kept from within the veil, but truly saw with their eyes the things which they had beheld with an eye of faith" (Ether 12:19): the blessing realized, the promise fulfilled.

Just as all blessings are the result of the laws upon which they are predicated, so the origination of bright and powerful ✺s is only possible in compliance with at least some, and often all, of the Eye of Faith Illuminants described below.

Brigham Young said:

> The greatest mystery a man ever learned, is to know how to control the human mind, and bring every faculty and power of the same in subjection to Jesus Christ; this is the greatest mystery we have to learn while in these tabernacles of clay.[9]

The Eye of Faith Illuminants are initiated by your divine spirit, and they are the key components of any ✺ upon which you choose to focus your Eye of Faith. At any given moment, the Eye of Faith Illuminants are essential to successfully focus your Eye of Faith and generate ✺s capable of thrusting out harmful and debilitating ●s.

The DESIRE Illuminant

This initial step may have already occurred in the form of hope, giving you a reason to focus your Eye of Faith. It is at this stage Alma says to: "let this desire work in you" (Alma 32:27). At this time you deliberately and purposefully identify an overall goal in the form of a sincere desire to achieve a righteous objective.

Be especially prayerful at this stage, to be sure your desire has the approval of your Father in Heaven. In honor of our agency, we are allowed to achieve objectives that may be detrimental, or not in our best interest or the well-being of someone we want to help.

---

[9] Brigham Young, *Journal of Discourses*, Vol. 1, pp. 46-47.

The PRECISION Illuminant

Because a desire is usually an overall generalization, precision is a very important Illuminant. I have found that many people hold a vague view in mind when praying, for example, and do not realize the importance of being exact and specific. We tend to rationalize using the assumption that because our Heavenly Father already knows what is in our hearts, we can simply generalize. For wise reasons, just as with the Prophet Joseph Smith, we must refine a general thought into a specific expression, an exact ✸ of the condition or circumstance we are seeking.

For example, a general ◯ of a tree allows many ◯s of trees to flash in and out of view, leaving the generalized ◯ hazy, unclear and uncertain. Precision or specificity is eminently significant. The more specific and precise you are, the more powerful the ✸. Therefore, refine the desire to a specific event, an actual condition, a particular action, a precise circumstance or the exact blessing you are seeking.

Illustration 14

The CALM YET ALERT Illuminant

Experience reveals that the level of calmness is a significant factor in the reception of inspiration and revelation and in the connection between the ✸ and the mortal response. We at times need to be reminded to: "be still and know that I am God" (D&C 101:16). Therefore, initiate a condition in which your body is relaxed and your mind is calm yet very much alert, attentive and responsive.

This is not to imply that you must engage in a relaxation exercise before prayer. However, a calm state of mind, free from agitation and contention, is obviously conducive to meaningful prayer. Learning to gain composure and control of our emotions, even when under stress, is a valuable asset worth the effort.

The relaxation step is a refreshing, healthful condition in which your thinking becomes free from the hustle of a busy day, void of obstructions and anxiety, to remain more clear and alert as you focus your Eye of Faith (see "Relax The Body and Calm The Mind" in Chapter 4, and "Eye of Faith in Personal Prayer" in Chapter 5.).

The FULLY REALIZED Illuminant

Because the mortal brain is inclined to interpret and accept messages from the divine spirit as reality, it is very important that the ☀ be as though it had already happened, as though it were already achieved or fully realized. The Nephite prophets labored diligently, "persuading them to look forward unto the Messiah, and believe in him to come as though he already was" (Jarom 1:11). Remember the example set for us by the righteous Jaredites when they "truly saw with their eyes the things which they had beheld with an eye of faith" (Ether 12:19).

The ☀ is the ideal way something would be if it had already happened. This is not wishful thinking, nor mere positive thinking and vain imaginations. Notice again an example of viewing into the future:

> Do ye exercise faith in the redemption of him who created you? *Do you look forward with an eye of faith, and view this mortal body raised in immortality, and this corruption raised in incorruption, to stand before God* to be judged according to the deeds which have been done in the mortal body? (Alma 5:15) (Italics added)

The LIFE-LIKE SIZE Illuminant

Many have a tendency, especially in their first attempts to focus the Eye of Faith, to see things as very small or tiny. Once again, the reality factor is important. Illuminate the ☀ in actual life-like size.

The LIVING COLOR Illuminant

The ✺ must be as vivid as possible. See everything in full color. See the colors in clothing, trees, grass, sky, furniture . . . everything.

The PROXIMITY Illuminant

Most people have a tendency when focusing the Eye of Faith to envision a ✺ off in the distance. It is important that you envision the scene in close proximity, such as only a few feet away from you, or as it would be if it were actually occurring. President James E. Faust counsels us: "As we pray, we should think of our Heavenly Father as being close by."[10]

The PERSPECTIVE Illuminant

You may assume an external or internal perspective. From an *external perspective,* your Eye of Faith may focus upon a ✺ in which you see yourself doing things and hear yourself saying things as though you were observing yourself from a few feet away. From an *internal perspective,* you will observe a scene from your point of view, or your vantage point.

The AMBIANCE Illuminant

The ✺ upon which your Eye of Faith focuses should be as complete as possible, and include the surroundings and the atmosphere of the object of your faith. A powerful ✺ will include a location, where you are, with whom you are, as well as what you and they are saying, feeling and doing.

The MOTION Illuminant

Our mortal lives are not occurring in a static motionless world. It is important, as you focus your Eye of Faith, to see the ✺ occurring in real time. For example, you may see lips moving

---

[10] James E. Faust, First Presidency Message, "That We Might Know Thee," *The Ensign,* January, 1999, p. 2.

when someone is talking. When striving to improve physical skills, motion is important. However, do not be overly concerned with this illuminant.

The CLARITY Illuminant

Keep the ☀ as clear and concise as possible. Envision all the details relevant to your intent. Remember, the ☀ will fade in and out. Do not let this bother you. Do not struggle to make the ☀ re-appear. Remain calm and continue, and you'll find that the ☀ will reappear.

The CONTINUITY Illuminant

Continuity is more important than clarity. See the action all the way through to the end. Even if the ☀ fades a little, as it often will, simply continue and allow the full ☀ to occur. For example, if you are saying a particular statement, be sure to say it all the way through. Once again, if the ☀ fades, do not struggle to make it reappear. Be calm and allow it to come back. It will. You can always repeat a ☀ as often as you wish.

The SOUND Illuminant

It is important that you hear the sounds associated with an event. If appropriate, hear your own voice and the voices of others in the ☀ upon which your Eye of Faith is focused. As Alma said:

> I say unto you, can you imagine to yourselves that ye hear the voice of the Lord, saying unto you, in that day: Come unto me ye blessed, for behold, your works have been the works of righteousness upon the face of the earth?" (Alma 5:16)

Instead of or in addition to voices, there may be other relevant sounds. Try to hear them as clearly as possible.

The EXPEDIENT Illuminant

Your ☀ must be (1) expedient unto the Lord, or (2) expedient for you, or (3) expedient for the person you hope to bless, or (4) expedient for the Holy Ghost to reveal, or (5) expedient at a particular time, or perhaps (6) expedient for a trial of your faith.

Moroni, quoting from his father Mormon, said: "And Christ hath said: If ye will have faith in me ye shall have power to do whatsoever thing is expedient in me" (Moroni 7:33). Moroni later recorded: "And Christ truly said unto our fathers: If ye have faith ye can do all things which are expedient unto me" (Moroni 10:23).

In that beautiful revelation designated by the Prophet as the "olive leaf . . . plucked from the Tree of Paradise, the Lord's message of peace to us," we are told: "Whatsoever ye ask the Father in my name it shall be given unto you, that is expedient for you" (D&C 88:64).

The Lord said: "Ask the Father in my name, in faith believing that you shall receive, and you shall have the Holy Ghost, which manifesteth all things which are expedient unto the children of men" (D&C 18:18).

With respect to time, the Lord cautioned the Prophet Joseph Smith: "Be patient, my son, for it is wisdom in me, and it is not expedient that you should translate at this present time" (D&C 9:3). The expedient time actually elapsed for Oliver Cowdery, due to fear, and he was told: "Behold, it was expedient when you commenced; but you feared, and the time is past, and it is not expedient now" (D&C 9:11).

In reference to Saints who remained faithful under the threat of mobs, the Lord revealed to the Prophet Joseph Smith: "I have heard their prayers, and will accept their offering; and it is expedient in me that they should be brought thus far for a trial of their faith" (D&C 105:19).

The TOUCH Illuminant

Although appropriate in only some circumstances, your ※ will be more "vivified,"[11] to repeat James E. Talmage's term, if it

---

[11] James E. Talmage, *The Articles of Faith*, pp. 96-97.

includes the touch of relevant objects. Examples of touch are described in "Eye of Faith and Temporal Endeavors" in the final chapter.

The REAL INTENT Illuminant

When you awaken and focus your Eye of Faith upon a ✺, it is important that you do so with genuine and real intent. Otherwise, as Moroni emphasizes, it profiteth nothing:

> For behold, God hath said a man being evil cannot do that which is good; for if he offereth a gift, or prayeth unto God, except he shall do it with real intent it profiteth him nothing.(Moroni 7:6).

In fact, it may be counted evil unto us if we pray without real intent:

> And likewise also is it counted evil unto a man, if he shall pray and not with real intent of heart; yea, and it profiteth him nothing, for God receiveth none such (Moroni 7:9).

Centuries earlier, the Prophet Nephi showed the importance of real intent in a summary statement of how to follow the Son:

> Wherefore, my beloved brethren, I know that if ye shall follow the Son, with full purpose of heart, acting no hypocrisy and no deception before God, but with real intent, repenting of your sins, witnessing unto the Father that ye are willing to take upon you the name of Christ, by baptism—yea, by following your Lord and your Savior down into the water, according to his word, behold, then shall ye receive the Holy Ghost; yea, then cometh the baptism of fire and of the Holy Ghost; and then can ye speak with the tongue of angels, and shout praises unto the Holy One of Israel (2 Nephi 31:13).

Real intent is a vital ingredient in every righteous endeavor, including the processes of repentance and forgiveness: " But as oft as they repented and sought forgiveness, with real intent, they were forgiven" (Moroni 6:8). In fact, real intent presupposes righteous intent. In the words of President James E. Faust: "Righteousness is a companion to faith. Strong faith is earned by keeping the commandments."[12]

In that unique and wonderful promise near the conclusion of the Book of Mormon, Moroni again emphasizes the importance of real intent:

> And when ye shall receive these things, I would exhort you that ye would ask God, the Eternal Father, in the name of Christ, if these things are not true; and if ye shall ask with a sincere heart, with real intent, having faith in Christ, he will manifest the truth of it unto you, by the power of the Holy Ghost" (Moroni 10:4).

The INITIATIVE Illuminant

Of all God's creations, men are

> ... to act for themselves and not to be acted upon" (2 Nephi 2:26). The prophet Lehi said: "And now, my sons, I speak unto you these things for your profit and learning; for there is a God, and he hath created all things, both the heavens and the earth, and all things that in them are, both things to act and things to be acted upon (2 Nephi 2:14).

Continuing this instruction to his son Jacob, who also became a mighty prophet, Lehi said:

> And the Messiah cometh in the fullness of time, that he may redeem the children of men from the fall. And because that they are redeemed from the fall they have become free forever, knowing good from evil; to act for themselves and not to be acted upon, save it be by the punishment of the law at the great and last day, according to the commandments which God hath given (2 Nephi 2:26).

As mortal beings quickened by our divine spirits, it appears obvious we should learn to take initiative and "act" rather than wait "to be acted upon."

The natural man is in a stimulus-response mode and therefore reacts. Put off the natural man.

---

[12] Faust, James E., General Conference, "The Shield of Faith." *The Ensign,* May, 2000, p. 19.

For the natural man is an enemy to God, and has been from the fall of Adam, and will be, forever and ever, unless he yields to the enticings of the Holy Spirit, and putteth off the natural man and becometh a saint through the atonement of Christ the Lord, and becometh as a child, submissive, meek, humble, patient, full of love, willing to submit to all things which the Lord seeth fit to inflict upon him, even as a child doth submit to his father (Mosiah 3:19).

We can choose to exercise control over the relationships between the spirit and the body, our relationships between ourselves and others and our relationships with our environment and our circumstances.

For example: Worry and anxiety occupy the mind automatically when you assume you have little or no control over an event or its consequences. Fear is the antecedent to faith. Conversely, as you focus the Eye of Faith upon a ✵, you assume control over mortal impulses and command the mortal brain, thereby increasing your capability to exercise faith. Otherwise, you are simply wasting your time in wishful thinking . . . and your faith is dormant. We are commanded to doubt and fear not by focusing upon the Savior: "Look unto me in every thought; doubt not, fear not" (D&C 6:38).

The EMOTION Illuminant

You must also try as much as possible to experience the feelings or emotions associated with the ✵ upon which your Eye of Faith is focused. You will notice the presence of emotion in Alma's description: "Or do ye imagine to yourselves that ye can lie unto the Lord in that day, and say—Lord, our works have been righteous works upon the face of the earth—and that he will save you?

"Or otherwise, can ye imagine yourselves brought before the tribunal of God with your souls filled with guilt and remorse, having a remembrance of all your guilt, yea, a perfect remembrance of all your wickedness, yea, a remembrance that ye have set at defiance the commandments of God?" (Alma 5: 17-18)

These words were spoken in warning to the members of the church soon after "Alma saw the wickedness of the church" (Alma 4:11) and resigned as chief judge in order to devote his full attention to the ministry. "Alma began to deliver the word of God unto the people, first in the land of Zarahemla, and from thence throughout all the land" (Alma 5:1).

Later in his ministry, Alma emphasizes the positive and vital role of "looking forward with an eye of faith to the fruit thereof," referring to that

> which is most precious, which is sweet above all that is sweet, and which is white above all that is white, yea, and pure above all that is pure; and ye shall feast upon this fruit even until ye are filled, that ye hunger not, neither shall ye thirst. Then, my brethren, ye shall reap the rewards of your faith, and your diligence, and patience, and long-suffering, waiting for the tree to bring forth fruit unto you (Alma 32: 42, 43).

The INTENSITY Illuminant

It is also very important that you feel with as much intensity as possible. In a revelation to the prophet Joseph Smith, the Lord chastised some of the saints for their transgressions because "In the day of their peace they esteemed lightly my counsel; but, in the day of their trouble, of necessity they feel after me" (D&C 101:8).

The saints were suffering severe persecution and now needed the Lord's help. However, when things were going well for them, "They were slow to hearken unto the voice of the Lord their God; therefore, the Lord their God is slow to hearken unto their prayers, to answer them in the day of their trouble" (D&C 101:7).

We must remember that in times of peace and well being, when everything is going well for us, we must still pray and exercise faith with the intensity we would if we were in desperate trouble, or dire need. This is not easy, but, especially when expressing gratitude for blessings, we should express our gratitude with the same genuine intensity with which we plead for help.

Moroni, writing of the Jaredites who lived centuries before his time, describes the power in the Eye of Faith to achieve a level of behavior at which

> there were many whose faith was so exceedingly strong, even before Christ came, who could not be kept from within the veil, but truly saw with their [natural] eyes the things which they had beheld [previously] with an eye of faith, and they were glad (Ether 13:19).

Imagine the intensity of a ✺ to generate a "faith . . . so exceedingly strong" they "could not be kept from within the veil," because they "truly saw with their (natural) eyes the things which they had (previously) beheld with an eye of faith" (*Ibid.*).

The illuminants described above are essential to keenly focus the Eye of Faith and open divine channels through which heaven-

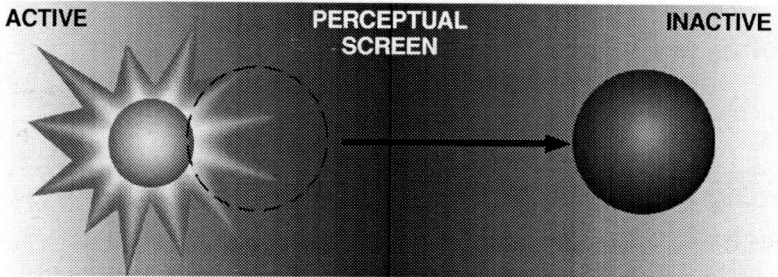

Illustration 15

ly power is manifest. In reality, when appropriate illuminants are observed, the Eye of Faith is (1) sharply focused and (2) a powerful ✺ is not only initiated, but, of prime significance, is (3) introduced directly into the crucial active domain, (4) bypassing our mortal limitations, (5) uninhibited by our physical senses and (6) unimpeded by our perceptual screens. Once in the active domain, the new ✺ (7) thrusts any and all relevant ⬤s into the inactive domain.

Furthermore, this fresh new ✺ initiated by your divine spirit (8) modifies the perceptual screen to (9) prevent related ⬤s from

Illuminating and Focusing the Eye of Faith

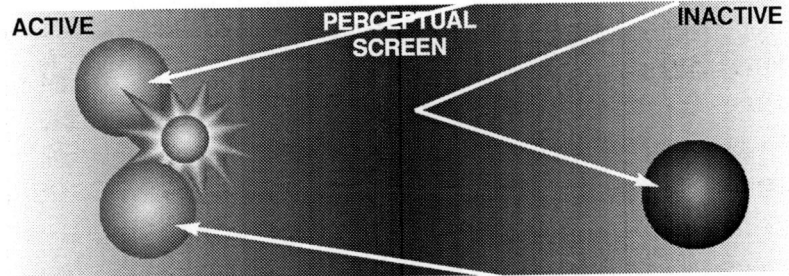

Illustration 16

entering the active domain and (10) to open the way for desirable reinforcing ⬤ to enter in the future.

Powerful ☀s may be generated in expressions of gratitude, requests for blessings in behalf of one's self or others, efforts to overcome weaknesses, fears and addictions, or attempts to achieve other noble and righteous endeavors. This supreme mental process produces unwavering faith to achieve all that is expedient to our Father in Heaven.

You will notice, all of the Eye of Faith Illuminants described above require focused mental concentration. Of course, our physical actions are also very important, but as the Prophet Joseph emphasized: "When a man works by faith he works by mental exertion instead of physical force."[13] We exercise our faith mentally and demonstrate our faith both mentally and physically. Alma concludes a concise summary of divine attributes with: ". . . and then ye will always abound in good works" (Alma 7:23-24). (See also Eye of Faith Hope and Charity, in Chapter 5.)

Although this magnificent mental process is initiated by "our spirits precisely as though we had no bodies at all,"[14] the mortal brain does serve a vital function as a source and memory bank of ⬤s from which we may generate our ☀s. This is why it so important that we retain as many true ⬤s as possible by reading the scriptures, including the words of latter-day apostles and

---

[13] Smith, *History of the Church*, p. 61.

[14] *Ibid.*, p. 34.

prophets, engaging in thoughtful prayer and living worthy of inspiration via the Holy Ghost.

ESSENTIAL FOUNDATION ✺S

Of all the recommended ✺s in this book, and those you will later customize for yourself, the following are the most vital, and the most powerful, and should serve as the foundation to all others:

1. ✺S OF GOD AS OUR LIVING AND LOVING HEAVENLY FATHER

Although we cannot fully comprehend His majesty and glory, it is important that we learn to open our Eye of Faith and envision Heavenly Father as a glorious being who loves us completely and unconditionally . . . a caring parent who understands our hopes and fears, our disappointments and aspirations . . . an omnipotent and omniscient being who tempers justice with mercy and assures that eventually absolute justice will prevail.

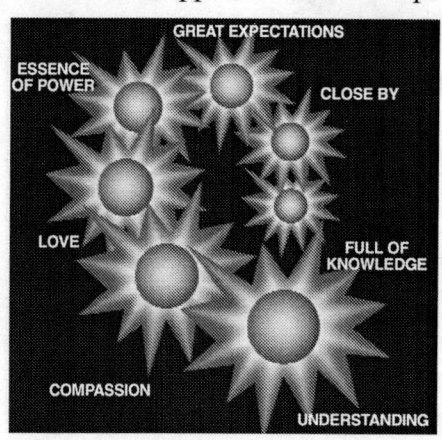

Illustration 17

Difficult as it may be to form a ✺ of our Father in Heaven, President James E. Faust recommends: "As we pray, we should think of our Heavenly Father as being close by; full of knowledge, understanding, love, and compassion; the essence of power; and having great expectations of each of us"[15] Notice the many ✺s suggested in President Faust's words. President Faust's recommendation also provides and excellent example of how a

---

[15] James E. Faust, First Presidency Message, "That We Might Know Thee" *The Ensign*, January, 1999, p. 2.

general concept may be refined into several specific ☀s. To begin, focus upon each attribute separately.

2. ☀ OF JESUS CHRIST
AS OUR EXAMPLE, ADVOCATE, REDEEMER

Before he became President of the Church, Elder Harold B. Lee wrote of a man who frequently asked himself what Jesus would do, such as "just what would He do in this given situation, or just how would He answer this question or solve this problem?"[16] That man in due time preceded Elder Lee as the President of the Church: David O. McKay.

President Ezra Taft Benson said: "What would Jesus do? or What would He have me do? are the paramount personal questions of this life."[17]

It is human nature for us to compare ourselves to others. However, asking such questions as those above when we make decisions helps us to compare ourselves to Him who invites us to "be even as I am" (3 Nephi 27:27).

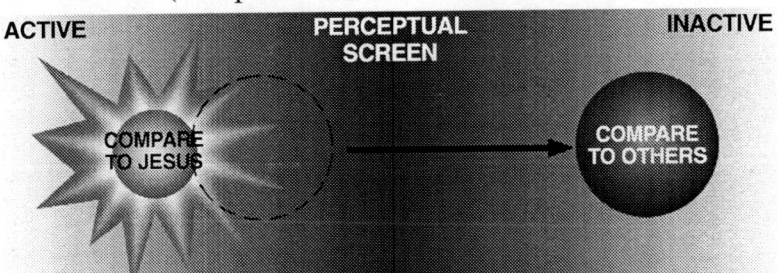

Illustration 18

It may seem to you that comparing yourself to mere mortals would be much easier than comparing yourself to a perfect being. This is not so. You will find, if you open and focus your Eye of

---

[16] Harold B. Lee, *Youth and the Church*, p. 49.

[17] Ezra Taft Benson, "Think On Christ," *Ensign,* April 1985, p. 13.

Faith on this possibility, and "see" the ☼ vividly and realistically, a sense of peace come over you, and you will assume a point of view of control. You will also find that this immediately brings a release from the pressure of worrying about what others think of you.

Just as it was necessary for Peter to keep his mortal eyes and concentration focused on Jesus, not the raging waves, to avoid sinking and to continue to walk upon the water of the Sea of Galilee, so it is necessary for each of us to keep our Eye of Faith clearly focused on our Redeemer, who said just before he invited Peter out of the ship: "Be of good cheer; it is I; be not afraid" (Matthew 14:22-32).

Yes, we most certainly do have reason to "be of good cheer" when we consider the infinite mission, the exemplary ministry and the incomparable attributes of Him who said "it is I."

In compliance with the Precision illuminant described previously in this chapter, you will find it very helpful to refine your Eye of Faith to specific events and circumstances in the pre-mortal, mortal, millennial and eternal life of our Savior. For example, you may focus upon ☼s of: "His matchless power, and His wisdom, and His patience, and His long-suffering" (Mosiah 4:6); "His goodness . . . His love" (Mosiah 4:11), "compassion" (3 Nephi 17:7) "and mercy" (Alma 5:48).

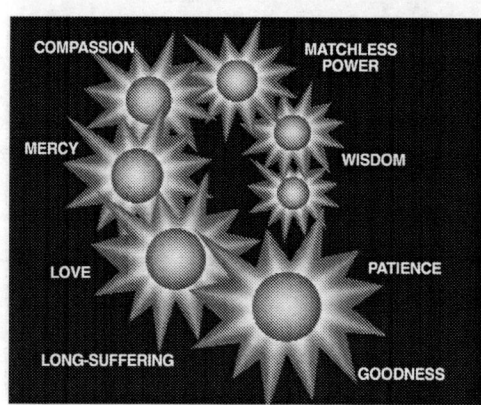

Illustration 19

In addition to the beautiful and tender ☼s above, it will also be very helpful to illuminate and focus your Eye of Faith upon ☼s of Him as the creator of worlds without number under the direction of the Father, as the literal Son of God after whose order is the Holy Priesthood we in our day refer to as Melchizedek, as the supreme pre-mortal being who spoke to and directed the affairs of mighty prophets as the God of the Old Testament, as our essential advocate with the Father and, above all, as our Redeemer who, at that crucial pivot-point when the direction of all mankind was determined in the Garden of Gethsemane and on the cross, was the only man who ever walked the earth with the requisite mortal attributes and the divine powers of a god to perform what He alone and selflessly performed for each and every one of us.

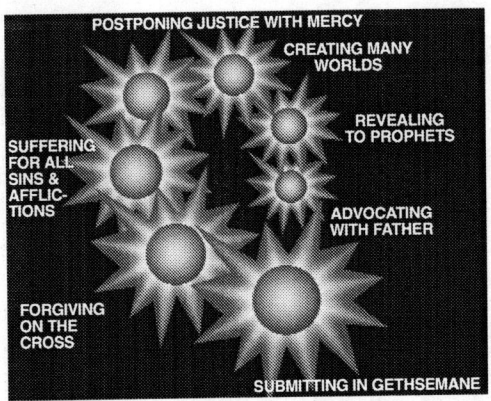

Illustration 20

Of Him and the infinite atonement, all of creation repeatedly testifies in many events and circumstances . . . many of which we may see with our mortal eyes . . . and of which we should learn to see the significance with our Eye of Faith. As we see the sun appear each morning from the east, may our Eye of Faith see ☼s of the Son of God returning in His glory. As we realize the earth is revolving around the sun as our source of our energy and life, may our lives revolve around the Savior and our Eye of Faith behold ☼s of Him as the source of our strength and the light of our lives. As we notice the green leaves wither and fall, and then return anew every spring, may we recognize through our Eye of Faith ☼s of the glorious and victorious aspects of the "great plan of happiness" He brings into reality. Even our going to bed at night and arising the next day may illuminate ☼s through our Eye of Faith to help us realize what He meant when He said: "All things bear record of me" (Moses 6:63).

Many typifying events occurred as Moses lead Israel from bondage to freedom, such as the manna or bread from heaven to sustain life, representing the Savior as the bread of life. Other typifying events occurred relative to the Book of Mormon, such as the plates coming forth from where they were buried in a receptacle, from which a stone was removed or rolled away, and all overseen by an angel. As Jacob testified: "all things which have been given of God from the beginning of the world, unto man, are the typifying of him" (2 Nephi 11:4).

As we focus the Eye of Faith on the supreme attributes of our Savior, we should intermittently shift our focus to our relationship with Him. We may do this by beholding ☼s of ourselves literally believing Him, believing His promises, trusting Him, remembering Him always as we pledge when we partake of the sacrament, loving Him with all our hearts, worshiping Him and acknowledging our dependence on His atoning sacrifice and redeeming power, recognizing Him as our perfect example, following Him by keeping the commandments and serving one another, and humbly and sincerely thanking Him in deep heart-felt expressions of gratitude. The brief moments we spend with our Eye of Faith illuminated and focused on ☼s such as these will translate into every waking hour of our daily lives and bring us closer unto Christ.

Illustration 21

To more faithfully heed President Gordon B. Hinckley's supplication just prior to leading the Hosanna Shout and pronouncing the dedicatory prayer for the Conference Center, "May we walk in the footsteps of the great Jehovah,"[18] our Eye of Faith must focus upon ☼s of where those footsteps have been, and where those footsteps are leading.

Oh, how numerous and mighty the possible ☼s—from His premortal Sonship, through His mortal Godliness, to His postmortal Godhood—of His POWER, of His WISDOM, of His COURAGE, of His LOVE!

3. ☼S OF YOURSELF AS A LITERAL CHILD OF GOD

This is one of the most exhilarating and significant ☼s upon which you may focus your Eye of Faith. This is a foundation ☼ because it includes acknowledgment and acceptance of a living Heavenly Father, the divine Sonship of Jesus Christ and our eternal potential by obedience to truth. Some specific attributes may include enormous potential, immense worth, obedient, divinely loved, faithful, forgiving and full of charity. You may think of others.

This ☼ is extremely important because it is capable of propelling you to higher levels of righteousness and service. Who you really are is an indestructible eternal being in a temporary destructible body. It is imperative that you recognize your real identity as your divine and eternal spirit, learning at this time to control a temporary and mortal body, in preparation for a glorious body of capabilities beyond your present comprehension.

Illustration 22

---

[18] General Conference, October 14, 2000, *Ensign,* November, 2000, p. 69.

4. ✹S OF "THE GREAT PLAN OF HAPPINESS"

During a long drive with a non-member colleague and our wives, he posed an intriguing question: "Dr. McIntyre, what would you do if you had ultimate control over your own world?" I quickly responded that I would teach everyone to be kind and loving toward one another, to look for ways to help and serve one another . . . and then I realized I was beginning to explain the Plan of Salvation. I took the opportunity to do a little missionary work, but for days I pondered that question and reflected upon the beautiful plan which is so comprehensive and promising in the Gospel of Jesus Christ, "the great plan of happiness" (Alma 42:8).

"Happiness is the object and design of our existence," declared the Prophet, "and will be the end thereof, if we pursue the path that leads to it."[19]

At the very heart of the plan of happiness is the invitation and the opportunity to become like our Father in Heaven. Among our most definitive resources for instruction on this subject are the seven theological lessons known as the *Lectures on Faith* prepared for use in the School of the Prophets and included in the 1835 edition of the Doctrine and Covenants. "Although profitable for doctrine and instruction, these lectures have been omitted from the Doctrine and Covenants since the 1921 edition because they were not given or presented as revelations to the whole Church" (D&C, "Explanatory Introduction"). Our Bible Dictionary we publish with the Holy Bible states: "The most complete and systematic exposition on faith is the Lectures on Faith."

From the first sentence in the first lecture, to the last sentence in the last lecture, the seven lessons articulate the great plan of happiness and accentuate the vital role of ✹s in the development and application of faith. Notice how often the Prophet emphasizes that they must be "established in the mind" and "planted in the mind."

---

[19] *Teachings of Joseph Smith*, p. 310.

The first two lectures explain the nature of faith and the essential role knowledge plays in the acquisition of faith. The last three lectures describe the Godhead, the need for sacrifice to produce faith sufficient unto salvation, the prophet's emphasis that when we work by faith we work by mental exertion, and the effects of faith.

Lectures three and four demonstrate the significance of some of the most vital *idea*s upon which we should focus our Eye of Faith: the characteristics, attributes and perfections of our Heavenly Father. They are, therefore, presented below to show the Prophet's acknowledgement that *idea*s are "essential to the exercise of faith."

Lecture Third

1. In the second lecture it was shewn how it was that the knowledge of the existence of God came into the world, and by what means the first thoughts were suggested to the minds of men that such a Being did actually exist; and that it was by reason of the knowledge of his existence that there was a foundation laid for the exercise of faith in him, as the only Being in whom faith could center for life and salvation; for faith could not center in a Being of whose existence we have no idea because the *idea* of his existence in the first instance is essential to the exercise of faith in him.

2. Let us here observe, that three things are necessary in order that any rational and intelligent being may exercise faith in God unto life and salvation.

3. First, the *idea* that he actually exists.

4. Secondly, a correct *idea* of his character, perfections, and attributes.

5. Thirdly, an actual knowledge that the course of life which he is pursuing is according to his will. For without an acquaintance with these three important facts, the faith of every rational being must be imperfect and unproductive; but with this understanding it can become perfect and fruitful, abounding in righteousness, unto the praise and glory of God the Father, and the Lord Jesus Christ. . . .

21. But it is equally as necessary that men should have the *idea* that he is a God who changes not, in order to have faith in him, as it is to have the *idea* that He is gracious and long-suffer-

ing; for without the idea of unchangeableness in the character of the Deity, doubt would take the place of faith. But with the idea that He changes not, faith lays hold upon the excellencies in His character with unshaken confidence, believing He is the same yesterday, today, and forever, and that His course is one eternal round.

22. And again, the idea that He is a God of truth and cannot lie, is equally as necessary to the exercise of faith in Him as the idea of His unchangeableness. For without the idea that He was a God of truth and could not lie, the confidence necessary to be placed in His word in order to the exercise of faith in Him could not exist. But having the idea that He is not man, that He cannot lie, it gives power to the minds of men to exercise faith in Him.

23. But it is also necessary that men should have an idea that He is no respecter of persons, for with the idea of all the other excellencies in His character, and this one wanting, men could not exercise faith in Him; because if He were a respecter of persons, they could not tell what their privileges were, nor how far they were authorized to exercise faith in Him, or whether they were authorized to do it at all, but all must be confusion; but no sooner are the minds of men made acquainted with the truth on this point, that He is no respecter of persons, than they see that they have authority by faith to lay hold on eternal life, the richest boon of heaven, because God is no respecter of persons, and that every man in every nation has an equal privilege.

24. And lastly, but not less important to the exercise of faith in God, is the idea that He is love; for with all the other excellencies in His character, without this one to influence them, they could not have such powerful dominion over the minds of men; but when the idea is planted in the mind that He is love, who cannot see the just ground that men of every nation, kindred, and tongue, have to exercise faith in God so as to obtain eternal life?

Questions and Answers on the Foregoing Principles

• *What was shown in the second lecture?* It was shown how the knowledge of the existence of God came into the world. *Lecture 3:1.*

• *What is the effect of the idea of His existence among men?* It lays the foundation for the exercise of faith in Him. *Lecture 3:1.*

- *Is the idea of His existence, in the first instance, necessary in order for the exercise of faith in Him?* It is. *Lecture 3:1.*
- *How many things are necessary for us to understand, respecting the Deity and our relation to Him, in order that we may exercise faith in Him for life and salvation?* Three. *Lecture 3:2.*
- *What are they?* First, that God does actually exist; secondly, correct ideas of His character, His perfections and attributes; and thirdly, that the course which we pursue is according to His mind and will. *Lecture 3:3.*
- *Would the idea of any one or two of the above-mentioned things enable a person to exercise faith in God?* It would not, for without the idea of them all faith would be imperfect and unproductive. *Lecture 3.5.*
- *Would an idea of these three things lay a sure foundation for the exercise of faith in God, so as to obtain life and salvation?* It would; for by the idea of these three things, faith could become perfect and fruitful, abounding in righteousness unto the praise and glory of God. *Lecture 3:5.*
- *What effect would it have on any rational being not to have an idea that the Lord was God, the Creator and upholder of all things?* It would prevent Him from exercising faith in Him unto life and salvation.

Why would it prevent him from exercising faith in God? Because he would be as the heathen, not knowing but there he might be a being greater and more powerful than he, and thereby be prevented from filling his promises. *Lecture 3:19.*

- *Does this idea prevent this doubt?* It does; for persons having this idea are enabled thereby to exercise faith without this doubt. *Lecture 3:19.*
- *Is it not also necessary to have the idea that God is merciful and gracious, long-suffering and full of goodness?* It is. *Lecture 3:20.*
- *Is it not equally as necessary that man should have an idea that God changes not, neither is there variableness with Him, in order to exercise faith in Him unto life and salvation?* It is; because without this, he would not know how soon the mercy of God might change into cruelty, His long-suffering into rashness,

His love into hatred, and in consequence of which doubt, man would be incapable of exercising faith in Him, but having the idea that He is unchangeable, man can have faith in Him continually, believing that what He was yesterday He is today, and will be forever. *Lecture 3:21.*

- *Is it not necessary also, for men to have an idea that God is a being of truth before they can have perfect faith in Him?* It is; for unless men have this idea they cannot place confidence in His word, and, not being able to place confidence in His word, they could not have faith in Him; but believing that He is a God of truth, and that His word cannot fail, their faith can rest in Him without doubt. *Lecture 3:22.*

- *Could man exercise faith in God so as to obtain eternal life unless he believed that God was no respecter of persons?* He could not; because without this idea he could not certainly know that it was his privilege so to do, and in consequence of this doubt his faith could not be sufficiently strong to save him. *Lecture 3:23.*

- *Would it be possible for a man to exercise faith in God, so as to be saved, unless he had an idea that God was love?* He could not; because man could not love God unless he had an idea that God was love, and if he did not love God he could not have faith in him. *Lecture 3:24.*

Lecture Fourth

1. Having shown, in the third lecture, that correct ideas of the character of God are necessary in order to the exercise of faith in Him unto life and salvation; and that without correct ideas of His character the minds of men could not have sufficient power with God to the exercise of faith necessary to the enjoyment of eternal life; and that correct ideas of His character lay a foundation, as far as His character is concerned, for the exercise of faith, so as to enjoy the fullness of the blessing of the gospel of Jesus Christ even that of eternal glory; we shall now proceed to show the connection there is between correct ideas of the attributes of God, and the exercise of faith in Him unto eternal life.

2. Let us here observe, that the real design which the God of heaven had in view in making the human family acquainted with His attributes, was that they, through the ideas of the exis-

tence of His attributes, might be enabled to exercise faith in Him, and through the exercise of faith in Him, might obtain eternal life; for without the idea of the existence of the attributes which belong to God, the minds of men could not have power to exercise faith in Him so as to lay hold upon eternal life. The God of heaven, understanding most perfectly the constitution of human nature, and the weakness of men, knew what was necessary to be revealed, and what ideas must be planted in their minds in order that they might be enabled to exercise faith in Him unto eternal life.

3. Having said so much, we shall proceed to examine the attributes of God, as set forth in His revelations to the human family, and to show how necessary correct ideas of His attributes are to enable men to exercise faith in Him; for without these ideas being planted in the minds of men it would be out of the power of any person or persons to exercise faith in God so as to obtain eternal life. So that the divine communications made to men in the first instance were designed to establish in their minds the ideas necessary to enable them to exercise faith in God, and through this means to be partakers of His glory. . . .

11. By a little reflection it will be seen that the idea of the existence of these attributes in the Deity is necessary to enable any rational being to exercise faith in Him; for without the idea of the existence of these attributes in the Deity men could not exercise faith in Him for life and salvation; seeing that without the knowledge of all things, God would not be able to save any portion of His creatures; for it is by reason of the knowledge which He has of all things, from the beginning to the end, that enables Him to give that understanding to His creatures by which they are made partakers of eternal life; and if it were not for the idea existing in the minds of men that God had all knowledge it would be impossible for them to exercise faith in Him.

12. And it is not less necessary that men should have the idea of the existence of the attribute power in the Deity; for unless God had power over all things, and was able by His power to control all things, and thereby deliver His creatures who put their trust in Him from the power of all beings that might seek their destruction, whether in heaven, on earth, or in hell, men could not be

saved. But with the idea of the existence of this attribute planted in the mind, men feel as though they had nothing to fear who put their trust in God, believing that He has power to save all who come to Him to the very uttermost.

13. It is also necessary, in order to the exercise of faith in God unto life and salvation, that men should have the idea of the existence of the attribute justice in Him; for without the idea of the existence of the attribute justice in the Deity, men could not have confidence sufficient to place themselves under His guidance and direction; for they would be filled with fear and doubt lest the judge of all the earth would not do right, and thus fear or doubt, existing in the mind, would preclude the possibility of the exercise of faith in Him for life and salvation. But when the idea of the existence of the attribute justice in the Deity is fairly planted in the mind, it leaves no room for doubt to get into the heart, and the mind is enabled to cast itself upon the Almighty without fear and without doubt, and with the most unshaken confidence, believing that the Judge of all the earth will do right.

14. It is also of equal importance that men should have the idea of the existence of the attribute judgment in God, in order that they may exercise faith in Him for life and salvation; for without the idea of the existence of this attribute in the Deity, it would be impossible for men to exercise faith in Him for life and salvation, seeing that it is through the exercise of this attribute that the faithful in Christ Jesus are delivered out of the hands of those who seek their destruction; for if God were not to come out in swift judgment against the workers of iniquity and the powers of darkness, His saints could not be saved; for it is by judgment that the Lord delivers His saints out of the hands of all their enemies, and those who reject the gospel of our Lord Jesus Christ. But no sooner is the idea of the existence of this attribute planted in the minds of men, than it gives power to the mind for the exercise of faith and confidence in God, and they are enabled by faith to lay hold on the promises which are set before them, and wade through all the tribulations and afflictions to which they are subjected by reason of the persecution from those who know not God, and obey not the gospel of our Lord Jesus Christ, believing that in due time the Lord will come out in swift judgment against

their enemies, and they shall be cut off from before Him, and that in His own due time He will bear them off conquerors, and more than conquerors, in all things.

15. And again, it is equally important that men should have the idea of the existence of the attribute mercy in the Deity, in order to exercise faith in Him for life and salvation; for without the idea of the existence of this attribute in the Deity, the spirits of the saints would faint in the midst of the tribulations, afflictions, and persecutions which they have to endure for righteousness' sake. But when the idea of the existence of this attribute is once established in the mind it gives life and energy to the spirits of the saints, believing that the mercy of God will be poured out upon them in the midst of their afflictions, and that He will compassionate them in their sufferings, and that the mercy of God will lay hold of them and secure them in the arms of His love, so that they will receive a full reward for all their sufferings.

16. And lastly, but not less important to the exercise of faith in God, is the idea of the existence of the attribute truth in Him; for without the idea of the existence of the attribute the mind of man could have nothing upon which it could rest with certainty—all would be confusion and doubt. But with the idea of the existence of this attribute in the Deity in mind, all the teachings, instructions, promises, and blessings, become realities, and the mind is enabled to lay hold of them with certainty and confidence, believing that these things, and all that the Lord has said, shall be fulfilled in their time; and that all the cursings, denunciations, and judgments, pronounced upon the heads of the unrighteous, will also be executed in the due time of the Lord; and, by reason of the truth and veracity of Him, the mind beholds its deliverance and salvation as being certain.

17. Let the mind once reflect sincerely and candidly upon the idea of the existence of the before-mentioned attributes in the Deity, and it will be seen that as far as His attributes are concerned, there is a sure foundation laid for the exercise of faith in Him for life and salvation."[20]

---

[20] Joseph Smith, *Lectures on Faith,* excerpts from *Lecture Third* and *Lecture Fourth.*

There is no better way to "establish in the mind" or "plant in the mind" each glorious and inspiring attribute that "gives life and energy to the saints" than to awaken the Eye of Faith and focus clearly upon the respective ✵!

ADDITIONAL ✵S ARE LIMITLESS AND INFINITE

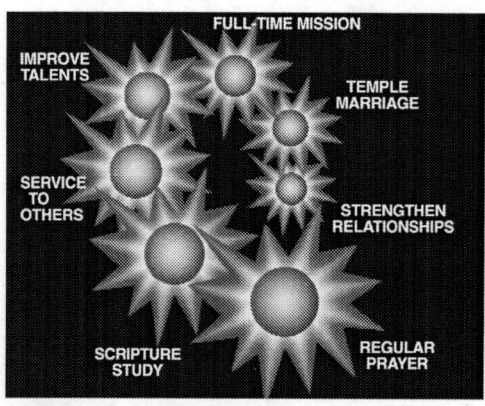

Illustration 23

The purposes for which you may open and focus your Eye of Faith are infinite, from the truthfulness of the Book of Mormon to the blessings of tithing, from the authenticity of living prophets to the benefits of the Word of Wisdom, from power in the Holy Priesthood to the reality of revelation. Among the most useful to you will be the many you are prompted to determine for yourself.

Our one central focal point, however, should remain the Atonement. Our future lives will be determined by the strength of our faith in the infinite scope, love and power of the Atonement. In one summary sentence: **focusing the Eye of Faith, according to the laws upon which its illumination is predicated, clarifies our comprehension of this doctrine of doctrines to the extent mortals may comprehend, which purifies us and enables our unconditional love in relationships with all members of the Godhead, all members of our families, and eventually all of mankind, and prepares us to live in light and truth and rejoice in the realities of the eternities.**

FOCUS UPON ☀S ANYTIME, ANYWHERE

Appointments are customary to visit a doctor, a lawyer, a teacher, a bishop, an auto mechanic, and even to avoid waiting at a restaurant. However, He under whose direction this earth was organized and all things are created, He who is supreme above all things, is available 24 hours a day, 365 days a year.

One busy morning, I said my prayers and went on my way. An hour or so later, in my hurry, I forgot I said them. I secluded myself and knelt down again. As I started, I realized I had said them. My first impulse was to apologize for taking His time again. Can you imagine?

Notice in latter-day revelations how often we are told to "pray always." (D&C 10:5; 19:38; 20:33; 31:12; 32:4; 33:17; 61:39; 75:11; 81:3; 88:126; 90:24; 93:49)

In addition to regular personal prayers, formal blessings, etc., you may awaken and focus your Eye of Faith anytime, anywhere, for whatever purpose you choose, in the form of a prayer in your heart, as the need arises: on the doorstep of a frightening assignment, in the office of an important business client, as you sit at the piano before performing at a recital, or as you confront your teenager whose behavior needs some understanding, yet firm discipline.

As you know, however, when your Eye of Faith is either closed or the view is dimmed or distorted—and your spirit, the real you, is allowed to shrink from your divinely endowed power of control—your undiscerning mortal brain, at any given moment, immediately and dutifully responds to "the natural man." At this point, although the spirit continues to enliven your mortal body, it assumes a subordinate role in your behavior and becomes "acted upon," to the detriment of both your mortal body and your divine spirit.

The following chapter is designed to correct the distortions, whether innocent or evil, that may be impairing the view of your Eye of Faith.

"For it must needs be, that there is an opposition in all things."
(2 Nephi 2:11)

4

CORRECTING IMPAIRED VISION OF THE EYE OF FAITH

When hope dwindles . . . when the scriptures appear meaningless . . . when prayer seems powerless . . . when depression sets in or transgression occurs . . . it is because ●s are prevailing and the Eye of Faith is closed, dimmed, or distorted.

For something to have power in one direction, it also has power in the opposite direction. To exert a force forward, an equal force must be thrust backward. It seems that the more potential something has for good purposes, the more it is able to be used for bad purposes. The automobile is a good example. With proper direction, it may be a helpful servant. Uncontrolled, it may become a destructive monstrosity. The examples of this fact are many. Perhaps some come to your mind such as television, movies, the internet and music. Because, as the Prophet Lehi emphasized: "For it must needs be, that there is an opposition in all things" (2 Nephi 2:11).

The mortal brain is, wisely, no exception. The capacity to reason inductively and deductively, to learn new things, to retain what we learn, to be able to recall it at a later time—all essential mental attributes enabling us to improve and advance as we should during our mortal probation, can and do operate to our detriment as well.

Many of our ●s in the active domain function in a range from useful and good through neutral and useless to levels of necessary hindrance that thwart our progress somewhat. However, many are literal ●s and exert very powerful, negative, destructive, even evil, though subtle, influences on every aspect of our lives. Some occur unintentionally, others are intentional, and all too many result from our exposure to ●s designed by those who, unwittingly, are "expert in the devices of the devil" (Alma 11:21).

DEVICES OF THE DEVIL

More than two thousand years ago, Alma and Amulek encountered "Zeezrom . . .a man who was expert in the devices of the devil" (Alma 11:21). If the adversary made expert use of devices then, may we imagine the extent to which the adversary uses modern technology to produce and distribute his philosophies today?

It isn't that all television writers and producers are evil. Nor are all magazine writers and editors, and everyone in the motion picture industry, intent on presenting only evil material. However, Lucifer has "exercised his power" in their professions in subtle messages that far exceed their intentions. Returning to that time about 82 B.C., Alma explains to Zeezrom that the devil "hath exercised his power in thee" (Alma 12:5).

Oh, how clever and cunning the evil one is in the absolute distortion of truth in the minds of millions today. These distortions and counterfeits of reality are powerful ●s that prevent good and decent people from recognizing the wisdom in the Word of Wisdom, from committing to a long-term marriage, from a state of mind receptive to inspiration, etc. This list could go on and on. There is no more powerful and sure way to counter these evil influences than to awaken the Eye of Faith and replace the ●s with ✺s of light and truth.

HAPPINESS: THE MOST DISTORTED

The Prophet Lehi summarized one of the reasons why our spirit bodies have been clothed in mortal bodies when he said: "Adam fell that men might be; and men are, that they might have joy" (2 Nephi 2:25).

The Prophet Joseph Smith expanded this saying:

> Happiness is the object and design of our existence; and will be the end thereof if we pursue the path that leads to it; and this path is virtue, uprightness, faithfulness, holiness, and keeping all the commandments of God . . . as God has designed our happiness—and the happiness of all His creatures, He never has—He never will institute an ordinance or give a commandment to His people that is not calculated in its nature to promote that happiness which He has designed, and which will not end in the greatest amount of good and glory to those who become the recipients of his law and ordinances.[1]

Because happiness is the object and design of our existence, Lucifer distorts happiness into ●s more than any other state of mind: material possessions, no responsibilities, popularity and fame, satiation of appetites, temporary thrills leading to lasting addictions. The list is endless, and the counterfeits of happiness are extremely deceptive and convincing. Although temporarily very pleasant and rewarding, they lead to pain, sorrow, failure and a life full of ●s!

DISCOURAGEMENT: A COMMON ●

In addition to the many counterfeits for happiness, the adversary persistently attempts to occupy our minds with discouragement, one of the most potent and damaging weapons against you and yours.

You have certainly heard of the suggestion to think of your problems and disappointments as challenges and opportunities, and that trials may be blessings in disguise. Just imagine the impact

---

[1] *History of the Church,* Vol. 5, pp. 134-35.

on your life if you really could, in the face of deep discouragement, immediately replace those depressing and dark feelings with bright ☼s of light and hope, and really see and feel the change. Not only would you suddenly feel different, you would also begin to react differently until reaction is overcome by initiative and you soon find solutions you would have never before imagined possible.

The results you will achieve by focusing your Eye of Faith demonstrate the fallacy in many ●s:

● #1—It's impossible because I know I'm unable to really change.

● #2:—It's not worth it, for even If I can change, it will take too long.

● #3:—What's the use anyway, I'm too old for it to be worth the effort.

● #4—I'm not willing because I would have to delve too much into my past.

The last one, #4, can be the most damaging of all. It is not necessary nor even desirable to delve into the past. Focus instead and completely upon refreshingly new ☼s. Thousands upon thousands of ●s, including many ●s, have formed during your lifetime and are influencing to one degree or another your self-image, your personality, your behavior and your spirituality. Although it may be well to recognize them, it is not necessary to delve into them and dwell upon them. In fact, some ●s are below the threshold of awareness anyway and not recallable, although they dwell in the active domain and continue to exert a detrimental influence on our lives. It is imperative, however, that you learn how to vanquish or replace them by properly focusing your Eye of Faith on new ☼s with the divine power to thrust even unknown ●s from the active domain (see Eye of Faith and Counseling LDS in this chapter.).

Illustration 24 shows specific ●s in a general ● of life being thrust from the active domain into the inactive domain as they are replaced by specific ✦s. When you take the initiative to focus your Eye of Faith on an appropriate ✦, the spirit knows what to do with the respective ●.

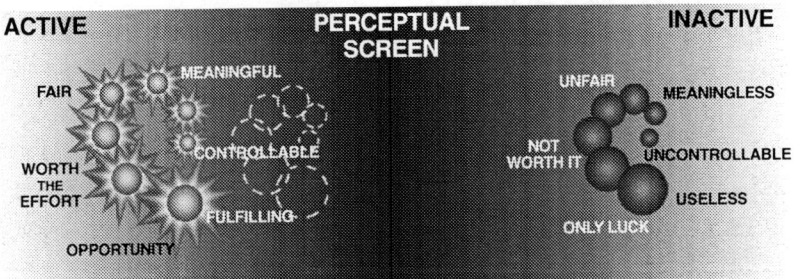

Illustration 24

MORTAL EYES and REALITY

During His mortal ministry, the Lord fully understood the perceptual nature of the mortal brain and its relationship to the spirit. He purposefully associated advanced concepts with many ●s of familiar perceptions such as sheep, salt, mustard seed, etc.

Illuminating your Eye of Faith is a function of your eternal spirit unimpeded by your mortal receptors. Serious misperceptions and distortions may occur due to the relationship between our mortal eyes and the interpretation of what we see by the mortal brain when the spirit is idle in the process.

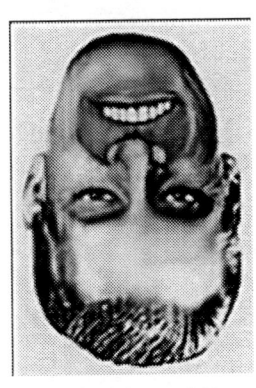

Illustration 25

Notice how easy it is to fool your perception of this upside-down face. Turn the face right-side-up and you will witness an example of how easy it is for the adversary to fool us when we are depending solely upon our mortal receptors.

Without being too technical, this misperception or distortion occurs because one portion of our brain interprets the over-all view of a face, and another portion attends to specifics such as mouth and eyes. In this example,

I have simply turned the mouth and eyes upside-down. When the face is viewed up-side down, that portion of the brain attending to specifics sees the mouth and eyes as normal, and thus the ugly view is not detected until the picture is reversed.

Perception is interpreting what comes in to us. Inception is organizing what we send out. Simply defined, *human perception is the process of interpreting sensory information.* Light waves penetrate the retinas of the eyes and sound waves stimulate the tympanic membranes of the ears. These and nerve endings of the skin, taste buds of the tongue, and the olfactory glands of the nose all send messages to the brain.

Many of our ●s and some ●s are the result of wisely placed physiological limitations over which we have little or no control. For example, we know that human eyes perceive only certain rays of the color spectrum because we are unable to see beyond the infrared and ultraviolet extremes at each end. Likewise, human ears are limited to a frequency range between 20 and 20,000 cycles per second (see Illustration 28 in Chapter 5).

Above are examples of physiological limitations. However, **much of our perception is a result of what may be termed psychological limitations yielding altered or distorted views of reality.** For example, because we are bombarded every second by such a large amount and wide variety of different stimuli, we are continually performing what is referred to as selective attention and selective perception. That is, because it is too difficult for us to process everything, we subconsciously screen out much of what would come to our attention. For example, at this moment, if you listen for it, you may hear a fan blowing, someone talking or some other sound of which you were totally unaware before you read this sentence.

Perception and inception are very complex processes and professional journals are replete with scientific terminology and theory. Suffice it to say, perceptions result from preconceptions of preconceptions of preconceptions, . . . etc. Likewise, our inceptions, our efforts to express our feelings, our needs, our hopes—

and our faith—are limited to our perceptual-inceptual database. Is it any wonder that we are continually admonished to study the scriptures regularly and prayerfully? Nothing comes from nothing, and promptings of the Holy Ghost cannot be received in a vacuum nor understood in a void. In fact, many promptings go totally undetected because our active domains are not even prepared to recognize them, let alone understand them. At any point in time, once we have properly inserted a ✺ into the active domain, we remain prepared from that moment to detect and respond, so long as we are worthy, at any appropriate time in the future.

POWERFUL ✺S ENGAGE AN IDLE SPIRIT

In the example of the upside-down face above (see Illustration 25), our perception is a function of our mortal eyes and the spirit was allowed to be in an idle position. That is, just as a motor in the idle or neutral position continues to operate, but without torque or thrust, so the spirit continues to enliven the body, but without direction or conviction. **Illuminating and focusing the Eye of Faith engages the spirit in a position of command over mortal thought by inserting powerful ✺s into the active domain, thereby releasing the spirit from the role of an idle witness to mortal distortions, adversarial counterfeits, and iniquitous deceptions.**

We have a tendency we refer to as human nature to accumulate debilitating and inhibiting attitudes about ourselves, others and life in general. Often it is said we subconsciously harbor these limiting thoughts in the back of our minds. Actually, they dwell in the active domain. Although we are unaware of most of them, they significantly control our lives because they directly validate the ●s in the active domain and modify the perceptual screen to allow even more ●s to enter the active domain. As this happens, the perceptual screen not only allows in corresponding negative perceptions, but it also rejects corresponding positive perceptions.

Although this natural process of the perceptual screen is essential, at least during our mortal lives, adversarial influences can and do continually take advantage of our human nature and distort truth to appear foolish and promote evil to appear desirable, directly affecting our behavior and our spirituality. It is not necessary to live with and suffer the consequences of these debilitating, distorting and limiting ●s in the active domain. We can thrust them out by correcting any impairment in the vision of the Eye of Faith and replace them with ✹s.

UNIQUENESS OF OUR PERSONAL ●S

In fireside situations, I ask groups of people to go to the window, look out to see what is there, and return to their seats. I then ask them to write down the main thing they saw. Invariably, with few exceptions, there are as many different impressions of what is out there as there are persons in the group.

One person notices a yellow car, another that the grass is green, and yet another that the grass needs to be mowed. Someone else from the same group will notice a bird in a nearby tree, while another's main impression will be that the sky is cloudy. Someone will say it's springtime and another will say a new building is under construction down the street.

Why do we see what we see? Why does one thing catch our attention above others in our view? Although many factors influence our interpretation of an incoming stimulus or an observed event, we already have our own unique view resulting from the content of our own personal active domain.

This personal and unique array of ●s and ●s in the active domain is a readiness to perceive our environment and our circumstances in a certain manner. An endless variety of origins may create our unique points of view because so many aspects of any situation may influence what we perceive.

Fortunately, the inherent power in the Eye of Faith sees through any and all such origins by circumventing the mortal receptors with fresh new 🔆s according to your own spiritual discernment and prompting from the Holy Ghost.

DISTORTED ⬤S and SINFUL CONSEQUENCES

Distorted ⬤s may lead to sinful behavior because they thwart a clear perspective of consequences. If, for example, a person really understood the consequences of a sinful choice, with an eternal perspective, a sinful choice would most assuredly be avoided. It all comes down to the accuracy, truthfulness or reality of what we do and don't perceive. Importantly, what we do and don't perceive is a result of the ⬤s, including the ⬤s, in the active domain.

In fact, Elder Neal A. Maxwell states

> Sin is a special form of insanity. It reflects a kind of blackout in which we either lack or lose perspective about the consequences of our thoughts, words, and actions. Thus, each of us in small ways (and in gross ways) loses our sense of perspective about the consequences of what we do. Often we wouldn't really hurt people if we knew the ultimate cost and price we all pay. Each of us remembers words we would recall and acts we wouldn't have committed if we had the choice to make again. It is that lack of perspective that causes much sin, although some transgressions are sheer defiance.[2]

In a later publication, Elder Maxwell asserts,

> So far as our real self-interests are concerned, sin is irrational even when measured merely in the dimension of time. It is insanity when viewed by the eyes of eternity.

When we begin to put off the natural man and move, however slightly, toward sainthood, we will find ourselves almost at once beginning to be stretched conceptually. It becomes possible for us to know things we did not believe it possible to know.[3] Being

---
[2] Neal A. Maxwell, *A Time To Choose*, p. 15.
[3] Neal A. Maxwell, *Notwithstanding My Weakness*, p. 74.

"stretched conceptually" enhances our capacity to comprehend, to envision and to recognize things of the spirit, things that are inconceivable to the natural man.

Distorted perception facilitates the commission of sin but, because of our agency, distorted perception does not force sin. If a person with a distorted perceptual view willfully chooses to see truth instead of distortion, the distortion may be replaced by the truth. A choice must be made. This is how sin is committed, and this is how sin is avoided.

There exists no more powerful way to correct distorted perception than to properly awaken, illuminate and focus the Eye of Faith. We thus begin to do our part to be "stretched conceptually" and become more eligible to receive "the things of the Spirit of God which the natural man cannot receive" (see 1 Corinthians 2:14.). "And now behold, my brethren, what natural man is there that knoweth these things? I say unto you, there is none that knoweth these things, save it be the penitent" (Alma 28:21).

REALITY of LIGHT and DARKNESS

I was privileged to attend the dedication of the London Temple during the time I served as a missionary in the French Mission. Just prior to pronouncing the dedicatory prayer to which the French saints were invited, President David O. McKay spoke about light and darkness in the human brain. He said as darkness is allowed in, an equal amount of light must leave. As light enters, an equal amount of darkness is dispelled. Darkness and light cannot occupy the same space at the same time. The only way darkness may be cast out is for light to replace it.

He emphasized that this exchange of light and darkness is voluntary. When we willingly search for fault in others, when we seek unrighteous dominion, when we choose to focus our thoughts upon wickedness, we willingly invite darkness in and thrust out that proportion of light. As darkness continues to enter, light continues to depart, and it thus becomes more and more difficult to comprehend truth.⁴ I will always cherish that experience, seated on the second row directly in front of the prophet. Thus we see, as darkness increases, our comprehension of truth diminishes. As our capacity for light and truth diminish, our ability to focus the Eye of Faith is impaired and our vision dimmed. Conversely, as we learn to purposefully illuminate and focus the Eye of Faith upon righteous 👁s, we invite in light and thrust out darkness.

The choice is ours. In the absence of light, darkness immediately occupies the void. However, in the encouraging words of President Boyd K. Packer referring to that choice and our agency, "ever and always light presides over darkness."⁵

"That which is of God is light" (D&C 50:24). This is the light that illumines the divine spirit and the mortal brain. Furthermore is the promise: "and he that receiveth light, and continueth in God, receiveth more light" (*Ibid.*). "And if your eye be single to my glory, your whole bodies shall be filled with light, and there shall be no darkness in you" (D&C 88:67).

REMOVING BEAMS FROM OUR OWN EYES

Of all the influences upon our lives, among the most significant are the 👁s we believe about ourselves dwelling at any given moment in the active domain. Everyone has them, although we were not born with them in the same way we were born with blue or brown eyes. They have been developing all our lives and form a composite of all our 👁s of ourselves and our 👁s of the way we believe others perceive us, right or wrong.

This process starts at birth. As we advance from infancy into childhood, the people in our lives tend to dominate our perceptions of ourselves. From family and friends, we learn more and more about who we are, how we look, etc. This happens whether the

---

⁴ (From the author's missionary journal).

⁵ Boyd K. Packer, "The Cloven Tongues of Fire," General Conference Report, *Ensign,* May, 2000, p. 9.

messages we receive are intentional or unintentional. It occurs whether the communication is vocal, in writing, in pictures, silent gestures or facial expressions. Unfortunately, our ◉s of ourselves result from false as well as true impressions.

As we enter the teen years and then advance into adulthood, other people continue to greatly influence them, including our friends and acquaintances, teachers, employers, fellow workers, husbands and wives, and even our in-laws.

At this point, in the removal of the beam from our own eye, it is important to distinguish between self-esteem and self-worth.

With **self-esteem:** esteem is the result of accomplishment. Confidence comes from performance. Service to others is self-centered for one's own benefit. Trust is in the "arm of flesh." Love is conditional. Circumstances and environment are in control. The frame of mind is short-term, here and now. One looks outward for validation which comes from the praise of others.

For those who seek self-esteem, behavior in a given situation is based on how they believe others in the situation expect them to behave. Then, because they behave in that certain way, others reinforce their expectation of them to behave in that manner. In turn, their expectation of how others perceive them leads them to act in such a way that they eventually develop in others the kind of perceptions they originally thought others had, and they begin to see evidence that they were right in the first place.

This begins a very dangerous reinforcement cycle, and the beam in the eye enlarges.

Self-worth, conversely, is the result of not so much what we can do, but rather who we are. Joy comes from service to others, whether anyone else knows it or not. Love is unconditional. Our point of view is long-term with an eternal perspective. It is our response to circumstances and environment that really matters. Our trust is in inspiration and revelation. We look inward for validation which comes from divine approval, not the praise of others.

Actually, we have all experienced the reinforcement cycle. That is, when we expect something to happen, we act in ways that increase the likelihood that our expectation will really happen. If it does, we assume the expectation was correct. This completes the reinforcement cycle and validates the expectation. Then that expectancy, whether it is right or wrong, becomes stronger and stronger as the cycle is repeated.

Unfortunately, and all too often, this cyclic action and reaction reinforces ●s that are distorted, outdated, harmful and debilitating. To be sure, the adversary takes advantage of this human tendency to reinforce ●s, further the work of darkness, and deplete our spirituality.

Fortunately, focusing the Eye of Faith, thus enabling the spirit to introduce righteous and desirable ✵s directly into the active domain, is the way to control the direction of the reinforcement cycle, deflate the need for esteem, and remove the beam from the eye. Powerful ✵s of yourself as a literal child of God, endowed with all the immense and numerous attributes this incomparable truth reveals, is worth every noble effort.

Therefore, realize who you really are. (You may want to review "Who You Really Are" in Chapter 2, and "Essential Foundation ✵s #3" in Chapter 3.) Placing your eternal spirit in command over your intellect, and thus over your mortal body, will reverse detrimental reinforcement cycles and set in motion a snowballing effect that results in an accumulation of uplifting ●s in your active domain. You will consequently experience more genuine beauty in your environment, recognize more good potential in others, love more unconditionally, serve more willingly, realize more happiness in your relationships, notice new horizons of opportunity, and generate higher levels of spiritual power.

MARRIAGE FAILURE and FAMILY DISHARMONY

Although marriages are breaking up and families are falling apart at alarming rates, I have seen marriages on the brink of divorce, rebellious teenagers determined to leave home, and a myriad of other relational problems make immediate and lasting reversals when the ●s were replaced by ✺s.

At the heart of our behavior is our perception, right or wrong. At the heart of our dilemma is our misperception, ours or theirs, or both. At the heart of our perception and misperception is the content of our active domains. Where contention prevails, many husbands, wives, teens and children are convinced the problems are someone else's fault. The misperceptions of who or what is to blame, and the roots of every episode of contention, disrespect, rebellion, etc. are the ●s thriving in the active domains.

It is said that we improve our relationships by using complimentary or affirming words, by touching in appropriate ways such as hugging, by giving our time or gifts and by serving. Commendable as these efforts may be, they are only effective to the extent they are perceived as genuine and sincere. Otherwise their effectiveness is only temporary and they will fail to bring lasting results.

Through slow-motion photography, for example, researchers have discovered what are termed *micromomentary expressions.* They happen so fast, our persistence of vision prevents us from consciously seeing them with our mortal eyes. However, we subconsciously detect them and readily respond to them. In fact, they exert far more lasting impact upon us than words because they are perceived as absolutely genuine and enter directly into the active domain.

There are more than seventy significant muscles in the human face, enabling a complex repertoire of configurations to produce more than a thousand different expressions and appearances. This wide variety of facial expressions is innate, not learned, and they are the same in different nations and cultures.

However, we cannot simply decide we are going to put on one or the other of a thousand choices for a certain effect we want to create. Facial expressions come from within and are only controlled by our true feelings and perceptions in a given moment in time. They must be genuine and they must come from within.

The most direct and immediate way to take command over our internal perceptions is to properly illuminate and focus the Eye of Faith and generate genuine feelings from within.

As we do so, powerful ✹s direct the brain to rouse motor neurons that relax and flex combinations of facial muscles to configure one or more of the hundreds of possible expressions. Those uncontrived but naturally spontaneous expressions will reflect our genuine expectations and communicate in a manner superior to any other approach. We thus perceive the hidden but true potential in others, potential unrecognized even by them, and thereby inspire that potential into full manifestation.

We have known for some time that, with respect to the emotional impact of what we express, words contribute less than 10%, vocal elements such as inflection between 30% and 40%, and facial expression between 50% and 60%.

Investigators in *pupillometric research* have found that even the pupil of the eye conveys meanings in a manner much stronger than words, in a manner that lasts longer than words, and in a manner that is much more believable than words.

For example, there are very subtle yet powerful meanings to pupil size. Regardless of light levels, a larger dilated pupil conveys more caring interest, affirmative expectation, encouraging attraction and an appealing appearance; whereas a smaller contracted pupil implies an uncaring aversion, negative expectation, discouraging repulsion and an unappealing appearance.

Once again, you are not able to simply dilate or contract your pupils at will. However, when you focus your Eye of Faith upon a ✹ of desirable conduct according to the needs of a loved one and the needs of the relationship, you generate genuine and sincere feelings and perceptions, your eyes and micromomentary expressions will so manifest, and your loved one will be invited, as never before, to favorably and willingly respond.

In addition to the subtle micromomentary facial expressions your spirit directs your brain to form at any given moment, your spirit also generates a powerful invisible influence that President David O. McKay referred to as radiation:

> Life is a state of constant radiation and absorption; to exist is to radiate; to exist is to be the recipient of radiations. Man cannot escape for one moment from this radiation . . . He can select the qualities that he will permit to be radiated."[6]

A more detailed account of President McKay's statements and descriptions of personal radiance are found in the following chapter.

As our personal spirits conceive reality by exposure to gospel truths, and then as we focus the Eye of Faith and introduce appropriate ☼s into our active domains, we not only improve our own lives, but we may improve the content of the active domains of family members and others by replacing ●s with desirable ☼s. We thus, in the most powerful way available to us, uplift them to the point at which they lift themselves out of bad habits, even addictions.

Remember, your physical facial expressions and the usefulness and scope of your personal radiance must be spontaneous and genuine to achieve righteous results. They must originate and emit from within. They do when you properly illuminate and focus your Eye of Faith.

We may be inclined to say to a teenage son or daughter whose bedroom is always messy: "you're so lazy and sloppy, no one will ever want to marry you." However, if we instead focus the Eye of Faith upon ☼s in which we see the teenager neat and orderly, happily maintaining a clean and organized bedroom, the results may be astounding for both the teenager and the relationship.

I know a parent who used the first approach for a year without any results. Then, after focusing the Eye of Faith and replacing

---

[6] President David O. McKay, General Conference Reports, April, 1950, p. 32; also in *Gospel Ideals,* Book IV, Chapter 22.

Os with ☀s, was cheerfully greeted about a week later by that same teenager saying, "I don't know why, but when I'm around you I just feel good and happy about being organized and keeping my room clean and neat."

Through your Eye of Faith you may see unrecognized potential in family members for improvement in any area of human endeavor, and sincerely relate to them through genuine micromomentary and other expressions as though they possessed those desirable qualities. You, in this manner, manifest genuine, sincere and unconditional love—a Christ-like love to which they will happily and gratefully respond.

Eye of Faith SEES the INVISIBLE and CHILDREN RESPOND

Students in my interpersonal communication classes often approached me outside of class for help with their personal problems ranging from drug addictions to pending divorces in their marriages. After hearing of the students' positive results, one of our secretaries asked me if I could do something to help her 10-year-old son who had been having very serious problems at school.

Her son's present and former teachers were so concerned about his personality and performance that he had been tested and found to be incapable of remaining in the regular school and would be sent to a special school in the district for problem students.

She explained that his problems were becoming increasingly worse. He would not respond to instructions in the classroom and refused to go to recess with the other students. Whenever he did go outside, he would not participate, and he sat on the ground as far away as possible. He would not talk to anyone and had no friends. He struggled with any form of homework, and teachers said he often had a blank expression on his face in class.

Although the mother and father had been warned in previous meetings with school officials, they were devastated this last time when they were told their son may not even respond to efforts to help him even in the special school.

She said she believed her son was capable of doing his school work, but no one could get him to do it. She was most concerned about his unwillingness to talk to others, his lack of friends, and apparent fear of playing with other children his age.

I had never faced a situation of this nature before with a person so young. I felt that if anything could be done, it would have to come from the mother and father in their relationship with him at home.

I asked her if she and her husband could really believe that their son could function normally. Could they really see through his current behavior and see his true potential? She said at home he was kind and responsive, but he immediately changed around others and hated school.

I asked if she believed he had the ability to do his age-level of academic work. She said he did things all the time at home that demonstrated he was intelligent and capable. She cried as she exclaimed: "He just won't use what he has away from home."

I then taught her a few of the principles of the Eye of Faith as I understood them at that time. She took notes and taught the principles to her husband that evening. The next morning she told me her husband was also excited about the possibilities and would make every effort to focus as clearly and sincerely as possible.

With hope in their hearts, they focused upon ✺s of their son willingly doing his homework, talking to teachers at school and joyfully laughing when playing with others during recess.

As they focused the Eye of Faith, wishful thinking gave way to a brightness of hope and then complete trust in a reversal in their son's behavior. In addition to spiritual influences, their faith materialized into micromomentary expressions (see Chapter 5) to which their son readily responded.

I was even surprised myself when only 10 days later she told me they were beginning to notice a definite difference in their son's attitude and behavior.

Five weeks after she first told me of her son's problems, his improvement had been so dramatic that she and her husband were invited to meet with several teachers and an administrator at her son's school. They had never before witnessed such a remarkable improvement in such a short time, and wanted to know what had caused the extraordinary change. The administrator explained that teachers and school officials were so convinced that their son was beyond help that arrangements were already underway to transfer him to a special school for such children.

Although I had no idea the results would come so soon and be so dramatic, I was not surprised by the fifth week because the mother had given me almost a daily report on his progress and the way he began to eagerly get ready for school in the mornings. He also began to tell his parents about his friends at school. The mother was especially pleased that he even told her the names of his friends.

Five years later, and four years after the mother graduated and no longer worked for us, she returned to my office to thank me again and tell me her son "is the best teenager ever."

Oh, how powerful the influence we exert on one another, for good or bad. Is it any wonder that, likened to the greatest of all commandments, we are admonished to love one another?

Eye of Faith IN THE DARKEST HOUR

For a variety of reasons known to the Lord, some blessings come only after we have entered our darkest hours, when our hope is dimmed to the very lowest level. "For after much tribulation come the blessings" (D&C 58:9).

I share a personal experience from which I learned a sacred lesson as a young Deacon that has become even more precious over the years, and has often been a source of unusual strength to me and may be of value to you.

After a day-long hike with friends up and down and across miles of foothills east of Cedar City, Utah, I discovered when

I arrived home that I had lost my wallet. The wallet was a special gift to me with engravings on both sides and a zipper closure.

We had hiked all day for miles across rocky terrain, jumped across dozens of ravines and slid down long gravely hillsides. Even if I could remember our exact route, I was convinced it would be impossible to see a light brown object from any distance, even if I accidentally passed close by the wallet.

Although I had little hope of ever seeing my wallet again, my mother reminded me of the power in prayer and urged me to take my loss to the Lord, with whose help, she emphasized, nothing is impossible if it is right. I was unable to begin my search until the following week. I left early in the morning and hiked in the direction I felt I should pursue.

It even seemed more impossible when I got into the hills, so I stopped and prayed every once in a while. I knew I could be miles from the wallet, and as the hours passed, my hope dwindled. After searching and praying all day long I eventually felt total discouragement. I looked out over the miles of sprawling hills, knowing I could not remember where we had gone. Everything looked familiar, because we had spent so much time in those foothills at other times.

I was heart-broken for two reasons: I could not find my wallet, and because I felt Heavenly Father had not helped me. I was exhausted and felt betrayed and defeated. If I did not leave for home immediately, it would become dangerously dark. The thought that my search was over and that I had to head toward home without my wallet left me devastated. I felt totally abandoned.

I began my search that early morning in compliance with some of the preliminary requisites to an opened Eye of Faith: my desire was strong, my hope was bright, my living was worthy, I was placing my trust in the Lord, and a simple ● of my special wallet must have unceasingly filled my point of view. But as the day wore on, my heart broke to the point of devastation, my hope dimmed to darkness, and I was about to nullify more than thirteen hurried hours of rushing along, wondering which hill to climb next, or along which ravine to search.

As I began to turn toward the city, my mother's words came unmistakably into my mind. Why again, I remember thinking to myself, had I not prayed and prayed all day? I would not pray again. I stood there with tears streaming down my face, thinking how strongly I did not want to pray. I will not pray again, not one more time, I said to myself, as feelings of bitterness mixed with my disappointment.

But for some reason, unknown to me then, I dropped again to my knees and poured out my heart. As I stood up from my prayer, I looked toward a nearby cedar tree. Near the foot of the tree, about 7 feet away from where I stood, my wallet came clearly into view.

Although my youthful faith was greatly strengthened at that time, my adult faith has benefited far more because I have come to recognize the true significance of what actually took place on that trying day many years ago.

I now realize the will to pray one more time did not come from me. Nor was the courage given to me to pray one more time only because I had done all I could do for myself. I later learned, from someone else, my mother had been on her knees on and off all day long at home, praying for me even more often than I had stopped to pray for myself. She faithfully retained ✺s of the Lord directing me, and lovingly maintained ✺s of her trust in me that I would not give up. I learned much later that it was her nature to pray often in this manner, raising three children alone, although unacquainted then with the term: the Eye of Faith.

This is a two-fold lesson of supreme significance: (1) there is great power in the Eye of Faith even if inadvertently applied in behalf of someone else, and (2) during those hours of frustration and disappointment, I was actually being guided all the time, through miles and miles of rugged terrain, to that very spot where rested my light-brown wallet against an identical color of beige shell rock at the top of one of the highest hills in the valley.

However, in spite of the fact I had been guided all day long to that exact spot, I would have missed my wallet completely, close as I was, had I failed to fall to my knees just one more time. And yet, at that very moment, in that very spot, I felt the most distress and rejection of all. The adversary did not want me to pray, especially when I was closest to the object of my faith.

How grateful I am for an unseen influence that helped me to my knees just one more time. That prompting I felt so strongly was the result of a faithful mother's Eye of Faith, opened brightly and focused clearly on powerful ✴s of trust in me, my endurance and perseverance, and faith in the Lord, His omniscience and omnipotence.

We must not allow disappointment, and that awful loneliness that may come when we think our Father in Heaven has forsaken us, to alter our path in life. Discouragement is one of the Adversary's most powerful tools. You will recall, it was when I was standing the closest to my wallet, the closest point to my goal, that I felt the greatest disappointment and abandonment.

It is often when the darkness is the deepest—when loneliness feels like total abandonment, when a relationship appears irreparable, when a goal seems unattainable, when an idea appears unworkable, when pain seems unbearable, or even when a lost item seems irretrievable—that we are at the threshold of the blessing. If we remain "faithful in tribulation" (D&C 58:2), and "patient in affliction" (D&C 31:9), and avoid complaining or "murmuring" (1 Nephi 3:6; 17:49; D&C 9:6), we may break through the darkness by keeping our Eye of Faith brightly opened and our view keenly focused.

We must not allow the Adversary to dim our Eye of Faith nor distort our point of view and lead us, discouraged, away from our righteous endeavors. It very well may be at the point of deepest affliction that we are closest to our objective. The adversarial weapon of discouragement is most powerful at the point when we are most vulnerable. Many miss the blessing because they give in or give up at that crucial period just before the blessing is secured and granted. Never give in. Never give up.

WORRY, ANXIETY, FEAR... OR FAITH

Fear is the antecedent to faith. The two frames of mind are bipolar and diametrically opposed to each other. Worry gradually allows faith to diminish. When your frame of mind allows you to dwell upon undesirable outcomes and you assume a position that the outcomes are only a result of chance over which you have no control, you are worrying and may be filled with anxiety.

Conversely, when your point of view is a vivid and bold ✹ of the desirable outcome, you demonstrate your faith and open channels to divine assistance beyond your mortal capacity. Hope may spring forth from even an absence of hope, and spark enough courage to generate belief that may flourish into unwavering faith.

...AND THE GLORY BE THINE.

Although the Lord makes it clear that "he that is compelled in all things, the same is a slothful and not a wise servant" (D&C 58:26), and that "men should be anxiously engaged in a good cause, and do many things of their own free will, and bring to pass much righteousness" (D&C 58:27), we must also remember that faith is a gift of God, and that He is the source of all righteous power (see 1 Nephi 10:17).

It is, therefore, important to maintain ✹s that visually include, according to your own situation, this acknowledgement: "... and the glory be thine." We must seek not our own aggrandizement but, rather, keep "an eye single to the glory of God" (D&C 4:5).

After all, He can do much more with our lives than we could ever do when trusting only in our own mortal abilities. President Ezra Taft Benson said: "Men and women who turn their lives over to God will find out that he can make a lot more out of their lives than they can. He will deepen their joys, expand their vision, quicken their minds, strengthen their muscles, lift their spirits, multiply their blessings, increase their opportunities, comfort their souls, raise up friends, and pour out peace. Whoever will lose his life to God will find he has eternal life."[7]

Eye of Faith MUST BE SINGLE TO . . .

During His appearance to the Nephites, the Lord counseled: "The light of the body is the eye; if, therefore, thine eye be single, thy whole body shall be full of light" (3 Nephi 13:22). Not only is this the same message He delivered to His disciples in Jerusalem: "The light of the body is the eye: if therefore thine eye be single, thy whole body shall be full of light" (Matthew 6:22), but He emphasized it during our latter-days in a revelation the Prophet Joseph Smith designated the "olive leaf:" "And if your eye be single to my glory, your whole bodies shall be filled with light, and there shall be no darkness in you; and that body which is filled with light comprehendeth all things" (D&C 88:67). Single to what? In the revelation above, recorded in the Doctrine and Covenants, the Lord specified: "single to my glory" and in Joseph Smith's translation of Matthew we find: "single to the glory of God" (JST, Matthew 6:22).

In the above counsel to disciples in Jerusalem, in ancient America and in our day, it is apparent the Lord's reference to "eye" is not our natural eyes. In the next statement to the Nephites, the Lord cautions: "But if thine eye be evil, thy whole body shall be full of darkness. If, therefore, the light that is in thee be darkness, how great is that darkness!" (3 Nephi 13:23)

Then in the next verse, the Lord explains that: "No man can serve two masters; for either he will hate the one and love the other, or else he will hold to the one and despise the other. Ye cannot serve God and Mammon" (3 Nephi 13:24). Your Eye of Faith must not only be single, but your focus must be upon a righteous scene. You cannot focus upon a ☼ and a ● simultaneously. It is impossible for you to perceive both at the same time.

---

[7] Ezra Taft Benson, "Jesus Christ, Gifts and Expectations." *The New Era*, May 1975, p. 20.

For example, in the illustration below, as you look at the blocks stacked in the corner, you may notice that one is missing from the top. Now, as you look at the floor, imagine that you are looking up from the bottom at a large group of blocks. As the scene instantly changes from one perspective to another, you will notice that it is impossible for you to see both at the same time.

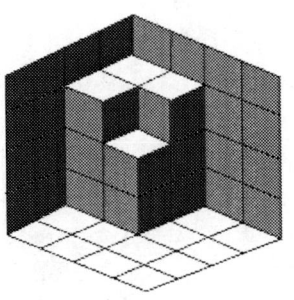

Illustration 26

You may perceive one or the other, but not both. You must choose. This is another reason why it is so important to learn how to focus your Eye of Faith and allow your eternal spirit to perceive a bright and vivid scene of a righteous ☀ which literally thrusts from your view any possibility of a dark opposing ●.

Eye of Faith and MISSIONARYING

Many investigators are willing to be taught the truth but, because of an addiction, will claim they do not believe something, such as the Joseph Smith story, rather than admit they are unable to live the Word of Wisdom. Others, although they feel sincere, may subconsciously be searching for excuses, faults or other reasons to avoid a commitment to pay tithing, pray openly before others, attend meetings, remain faithful, etc.

All human beings come into mortality with the potential to eventually see with an Eye of Faith, unless there are certain rare forms of brain deficiency or damage. In most, however, the Eye of Faith is merely closed or asleep. In others, the Eye of Faith is awake but dim and out of focus. In yet many others, the Eye of Faith is focused, but only upon distorted and false ●s which are in reality forcefully detrimental, harmful and debilitating ●s.

Let's consider an investigator who intends to read the Book of Mormon to determine its truthfulness. In many cases, a genuine desire may already exist, hope may be at a high level, and the investigator may read with a sincere heart and real intent to genuinely discover the truth.

In many other circumstances, however, we find investigators who are heavy smokers, for example, and yet well aware of prerequisites to baptism, including observance of the Word of Wisdom. For such a person, when reading the Book of Mormon to assess its truthfulness, a genuine desire to really discover that the record is true, a sincere hope that it is indeed the word of God, may be difficult to achieve; not because they fail to read it carefully, even prayerfully, but because they realize that if the Book of Mormon is true, they must stop smoking. This realization, even though they may not be aware of it, originates a subtle ● that blocks the "sincere heart" and "real intent" admonished by Moroni (Moroni 10:4). This occurs even though they may feel they are really reading with sincerity and real intent. The awareness that there must be a willingness to stop smoking harbors a view down deep of a ● that the book is really not true, so they can continue in the addiction. This is true with all addictions and all unacceptable behavior requiring repentance before baptism.

Helping investigators to properly focus the Eye of Faith may not only be one of the most powerful ways, but may be the only way the heart and mind will open to receive the witness of the Holy Ghost.

Some investigators will be unaware that they actually harbor a deceptive ● in a hope that the Gospel is not true, so they may continue to go boating on Sundays, or engage in whatever, etc. Although at a subconscious level, ●s of this nature will block channels of divine communication.

Investigators facing these common but serious dilemmas may be helped to obey the laws upon which specific blessings are predicated by observing the Eye of Faith illuminants and the Essential Foundation ✵s in Chapter 3. By so doing, they will focus the Eye of Faith on a willingness to forsake the habit and "give away all" as did King Lamoni's repentant father (Alma 22:18), and with a "sincere heart" and with "real intent" invite the enabling power of the Holy Ghost to open the way to victory over any addiction, phobia or inhibition. As righteous ☼s are generated in this effort, competing ●s are relegated to the inconsequential domain and a sincere heart and real intent emerge, opening the channel for the Holy Ghost to bear witness and manifest the truthfulness thereof.

As the missionary, you must humbly and prayerfully seek divine inspiration in order to suggest appropriate ☼s upon which the investigator may focus his or her Eye of Faith. Always remember, the Holy Ghost already knows the nature of the investigator's ●s.

You may be working with an investigator who is unable to focus the Eye of Faith for one reason or another. When this happens, use the principles described in "Strengthening the Eye of Faith in this chapter.

The experiences of two young men are described in the last chapter who overcame personal problems by focusing the Eye of Faith. They were both called to serve full-time missions soon thereafter and taught some of the Eye of Faith illuminants to investigators in the mission field who were thus able to successfully overcome addictions and live the Word of Wisdom in preparation for baptism.

Eye of Faith and COUNSELING LDS

As a missionary in France only 13 years after the close of WWII, I was often met at the door by someone who had witnessed so much destruction and unfair suffering, even by innocent children, they insisted there could be no God. In one war-torn village, the residents decided the rebuilding should begin at the central plaza where fragments of a statue of the Christus lay scattered amidst the rubble. They were able to reassemble the statue, piece-by-piece, all except the hands. Without hands, some thought the statue should be removed from the plaza. For tradition sake, however, it was finally decided to leave the statue there. After thoughtful consideration a plaque was made and attached to the base of the Christus which read: "Je n'ai pas les mains sauf les vôtres," meaning "I have no hands but yours."

Our Father in Heaven wisely provides for our growth and development by allowing us to use our own hands in behalf of one another, to help one another become capable of helping ourselves.

If you have the opportunity to be in a position in which you are to advise and counsel others, by virtue of a church calling, your profession, or as a family member or friend, consider how hands may help other hands to help themselves by learning to awaken and focus the Eye of Faith, yours and theirs.

The feelings of people I encountered in the war-torn areas of France, who suffered and survived, may have been similar to Mormon's feelings as he describes this panoramic view after recounting the story of the people of Ammon: " and thus we see the great reason of sorrow, and also of rejoicing—sorrow because of death and destruction among men, and joy because of the light of Christ unto life" (Alma 28:14).

When the Eye of Faith is focused, we clearly distinguish the dichotomies at the two extremes of this continuum, as did Alma, between despair and hope, between deception and truth, between sin and righteousness, between darkness and light, between sorrow and joy.

However, when a Latter-day Saint's Eye of Faith is dimmed or distorted for one reason or another, the restrictive and yet essential functions of the perceptual screen may have allowed a strong ● to replace a weaker ● in the active domain.

We begin to assist others to help themselves by purposefully focusing our own Eye of Faith. Always remember, no matter how offensive he or she may be to you, try with all your might to focus your own Eye of Faith upon this person in such a way that you see him or her, not as a doubter, not as a belligerent criticizer, not as a rationalizer and not as evil, but as someone seeking to do what is right and seeking for the truth. Your mortal intellect may tell you they are just not worth it. It's their own fault, etc. Don't let yourself dwell on these things. Focus clearly on their potential to sincerely want to do what is right. It is in them. To help them, you must see that potential. As you treat them as seekers after truth, they will feel your love for them. To see that potential, you must focus your own Eye of Faith. See them as a "child of God." You will thus treat them as though they had those desirable qualities, and you will bring those qualities to life, and they will begin to feel and then behave as though they do indeed have those qualities.

Make no suggestions and offer no counsel at this point. Listen carefully. As you listen, ask yourself two vital questions, the second of which is by far the most important: (1) What are the prevailing ⬤s, and (2) what should be the scope and content of the ✹s?

Keep in mind, however, if we are to help someone to help themselves, it is not the ⬤s upon which we should dwell, but rather the origination of a powerful new ✹ capable of thrusting the respective harmful ⬤ from the active domain.

Perhaps the person you are helping feels as did Korihor: "And thus ye lead away this people after the foolish traditions of your fathers, and according to your own desires . . . that they durst not look up with boldness, and that they durst not enjoy their rights and privileges. . . . and have brought them to believe, by their traditions and their dreams and their whims and their visions and their pretended mysteries, that they should, if they did not do according to their words, offend some unknown being, who they say is God—a being who never has been seen or known, who never was nor ever will be" (Alma 30:2-28).

One may see fault in a Bishop, an auxiliary leader, a parent, etc., and thus doubt the Gospel or find fault with the Church. Another may know very well the principles of the Gospel, and yet be subject to a ⬤ that fails to recognize the truthfulness of those very principles. One may be disappointed or confused by an event or a circumstance because their view of such is impaired. Another may be looking for an excuse to indulge in certain behaviors or engage in certain activities. One may be belligerently looking for fault and thus, in reality, unwittingly generate multiple ●s that support and reinforce the rationalization.

Such distortions of view may cause those who have generated these and other ●s to perceive scriptural discrepancies in the writings of ancient prophets, or contradictions by living prophets.

Perhaps their feelings and doubts are the result of false or proud ●s similar to those of Martin Harris, of whom the Lord said:

> Behold, I say unto him, he exalts himself and does not humble himself sufficiently before me; but if he will bow down before me, and humble himself in mighty prayer and faith, in the sincerity of his heart, then will I grant unto him a view of the things which he desires to see (D&C 5:24).

In most cases, members with these problems are still looking for something with their natural eyes rather than the Eye of Faith, as Alma understood: "Yea, there are many who do say: If thou wilt show unto us a sign from heaven, then we shall know of a surety; then we shall believe" (Alma 32:17).

One's Eye of Faith may be completely closed or wholly out of focus. Another may have good intentions, but have no idea upon what to focus, and yet another may be unable to focus at all.

Be aware of what I call the "hardness-to-blindness-to-hardness cycle." What is the condition of the heart? Hardness of heart dims the Eye of Faith. Continual hardness of heart leads to blindness of the Eye of Faith.

Conversely, opening and focusing the Eye of Faith softens the heart. As the heart softens, it becomes much easier to focus the Eye of Faith. As the focusing continues, the softening continues. As the softening continues, focusing improves, "and their scales of darkness shall begin to fall from their eyes" (2 Nephi 30:6). Oh, how important it is that you help them to awaken and focus their own Eye of Faith!

Once again, dwell not on the ●, but rather focus your time and attention on what should be the composition of the ✹.

Make no decisions for them. Members are encouraged to make a diligent effort, including earnest prayer and scripture study, to solve their own problems. However, if you are appropriately involved, as a friend or family member, as a professional or an authorized church leader entitled to discernment and inspiration as a spiritual advisor, you may feel prompted to help them understand and apply some or all of the Eye of Faith illuminants described in Chapter 3. It is important that they know how to focus the Eye of Faith. Once they are able to focus clearly, they should begin with the "Essential Foundation ✸s also presented in Chapter 3.

It may be necessary, and you may feel prompted to help them as they determine the composition of their ✸s. However, to the extent they are able to do, help them to seek their own inspiration as they originate their own ✸s.

In this manner, as they seek the promptings of the Holy Ghost in identifying or composing the content of their own ✸s, upon which they focus their Eye of Faith, they become more "spiritually self-reliant." President Boyd K. Packer acknowledges that: "The Lord is very generous with the freedom He gives us. The more we learn to follow the right, the more we are spiritually self-reliant, the more our freedom and our independence are affirmed."[8] The Lord said, "If ye continue in my word, then are ye my disciples indeed; And ye shall know the truth, and the truth shall make you free" (John 8:31-32).

As they learn to focus the Eye of Faith and determine the composition of their own ✸s, help them to select a focal point on the well-being of others. As they concentrate more on others and less on themselves, the capacity for charity increases. As the capacity for charity increases, hope is brightened and faith is strengthened, resulting in good works and an enlargement of the capacity for charity.

This loving and selfless cyclical process generates an upward spiral, described and illustrated in the next chapter, and results in

---

[8] Boyd K. Packer, *Teach Ye Diligently,* p. 207.

the sought-for conditions of solving, healing, overcoming, improving, vanquishing, conquering, achieving and serving.

SEEING THINGS AS THEY REALLY ARE

Why does one teenager see someone with a cigarette in the mouth as "neat" or "cool," while another teenager sees the same scene as ridiculous and foolish? Oh, the paramount significance of the contents of the active domain, the destructive distortions of ●s, and the triumphant dominance of powerful ✺s resulting from a righteously focused Eye of Faith!

When we learn to control the "eye" through which we really behold, we will have acquired a two-fold attribute, both mortal and spiritual, of immeasurable potential and remarkable power.

When Jacob wrote "of things as they really are, and of things as they really will be," he was referring to the reality or truth that comes from the "spirit" and the fact that it comes "plainly" (Jacob 4:13). Then in the next verse, he refers to those who "despised the words of plainness . . . because of their blindness" (Jacob 4:14).

The "blindness" may be overcome by awakening the Eye of Faith. Our degree of readiness to perceive truth, and accept it, determined by the ● in the active domain, is the degree to which we will be able to distinguish between truth and error, and apply truth day-to-day living.

In every realm of our lives, we must learn to properly focus the Eye of Faith upon ✺s that amend the ●s in the active domain to an eternal perspective.

On the same evening, two people may see the same radiant sunset from the same vantage point. One will experience a deep sense of beauty. The other may be totally oblivious to anything more than the fact it is evening. Two people may read the same passage of scripture. One will recognize an application for his or her life. The other may be unaware of any application whatsoever. The difference is in the ●s, including the ●s, in the active domain.

Why is perceptual accuracy so important? Why are clear concepts of truth so vital? Why is an eternal perspective so crucial? Because, at any age, blurred and distorted perception, results in a downward cycle of irrational thought and irrational behavior. Reacting to misperceptions of reality and distortions of truth undermine, if not annihilate, the very foundations of faith. We must learn to strengthen the Eye of Faith.

STRENGTHENING THE Eye of Faith

It has been my experience that many Latter-day Saints, and people in general, find it difficult, and some find it impossible, to clearly envision something ... to engage their divine spirit in that meaningful relationship with the cerebral cortex portion of their brain that must occur for the Eye of Faith to meaningfully illuminate and clearly focus. They experience difficulty advancing from belief to total trust and unwavering faith, because the object of their faith is uncertain, ambiguous, distorted, weak, or out of focus.

As we made the transition from pre-mortal existence to this mortal life, a veil between the two realms enables us to live by faith and accomplish the purposes for which we came to earth because our mortal brains are unaware of the knowledge our individual spirits possess of pre-mortal experiences.

Until we approach eight years of age, we are in a stage of perceptual innocence. That is, we have few preconceived notions of what life should be. We are in awe and wonderment, and delight in discovery and limitless possibilities. This innocent, unburdened and trusting time may include some of the reasons the Savior said on at least two continents that we must "become as a little child" (3 Nephi 11:37-38; Matthew 18:3).

If you found it difficult to apply any of the Eye of Faith illuminants in the last chapter, be assured that the difficulty lies not in an incapability of your spirit, for the spirit is capable, but rather in one or a number of mortal tendencies and characteristics.

The following sections, therefore, explain significant characteristics of the mortal brain relevant to its relationship to the divine spirit:

CEREBRAL HEMISPHERIC DIFFERENCE

We have learned a lot in recent years about the duel nature of the human brain. It has two very different yet related sides or hemispheres connected by a membrane called the corpus callosum. Each hemisphere presides over different functions too numerous to itemize here. It is helpful to realize, however, that the left side comprehends sequentially and, for example when reading, recognizes the words. The right side comprehends simultaneously and, when reading, envisions the ideas.

To enable the saints in firesides and participants in seminars to experience the difference between the two hemispheres, I ask them to say the colors they see on a screen as soon as the colors appear They break into laughter before they even see the third color because the right and left hemispheres of the brain counteract each other as one side recognizes the words and the other recognizes the colors in a special visual sequence.

Considering hemispheric differences is important because focusing the Eye of Faith is so dependent upon a healthy and active right hemisphere.

CEREBRAL HEMISPHERIC BALANCE

Both cerebral hemispheres are essential and should be somewhat in balance and able to communicate with each other. However, the right side in most of us, from the teens on up, is underdeveloped. Research has revealed that children are fully developed on both sides, but as the years go by, because adults spend the majority of their waking hours using the left brain, the right brain begins to weaken. And too, our educational system and our socialization process tend to stress left hemisphere learning. The visual right hemisphere begins to atrophy and becomes almost dormant. We now know to be happier, healthier, and more successful, we must strengthen the right hemisphere wherein dwells the capacity to foresee or anticipate the results of a particular action. Difficulty focusing the Eye of Faith is often the result of an atrophied but correctable right hemisphere.

CEREBRAL HEMISPHERIC HARMONY

For many people, over-use of the left side, because the right side is stifled, leads to stress, negativity, emotional instability, depression and anxiety. These conditions and a tendency toward addictive behaviors such as over-eating, smoking and drug abuse result when the right side is either underdeveloped or when the two sides are not working in harmony.

Focusing the Eye of Faith can correct this right brain dysfunction and diffuse the emotional reaction. We must develop the right hemisphere, and we must help the two hemispheres to interact in a positive, supporting way. Although the right side may be underdeveloped and under little control, it still dominates our emotions and the relationship between the spirit and the body.

EXERCISE THE RIGHT HEMISPHERE

As explained above, many people find it difficult, and some find it almost impossible, to clearly and purposefully envision something, to perceive or anticipate a desirable outcome or the results of a certain course of action. They remain unable to put Alma's experiment to the test. They thus experience difficulty advancing from belief to total trust and unwavering faith, because the object of their faith is dim, blurred, or ambiguous. That vital relationship between the divine spirit and the cerebral cortex of the mortal brain is impaired.

The most effective and beneficial way to strengthen the right hemisphere, achieve balance and harmony between the two hemispheres and thereby improve the ability to focus the Eye of Faith is to read the scriptures, including the words of living Apostles and prophets, in the following manner: apply as many of the Eye of Faith illuminants as possible or appropriate to focus upon ✺s of the authors in their desires to describe truth to you and ✺s of the situations and circumstances in the descriptions, and then, most importantly, ✺s likening the principles to yourself in vivid ✺s of direct applications in your daily life, with family members, with friends and associates, at school and at work, in church callings and in service to others.

Illuminating and focusing your Eye of Faith upon such ✺s will powerfully exercise the visio-conceptual regions so vital to clarity and focus. You will not only experience an increase in your comprehension of everlasting truths, but you will dramatically expand your capability to focus your Eye of Faith and observe eternal principles beyond the limitations of your mortal eyes.

Strengthening the right hemisphere and bringing it into balance is also extremely important in the achievement of our goals. Research investigators have found—just prior to an expert marksman pulling the trigger, a golfer striking the ball, an archer releasing the arrow, or a basketball player in the final motion of shooting the basketball—the right side of the brain erupts in a burst of activity. The frequency of brain waves on the left side, however, is reduced. This does not happen with amateurs. It only happens after many months of training. Also, by pinpointing the cells in the brain most active during peak performance, two areas on the right side were discovered that dramatically increase during intense concentration.

Another reason for which we should strengthen the right side is the fact that, when we begin to learn a new skill, many different areas of the brain are active simultaneously. But, as we practice, the brain begins to fine-tune specific neural circuits involved in the process. Then, as we become more proficient, brain activity becomes more focused on the circuits directly involved in producing the result. Awakening and focusing the Eye of Faith expedites this process in areas throughout the brain as the divine spirit assumes control over the mortal body.

RELAX THE BODY AND CALM THE MIND

Returning to the differences between the left and right hemispheres of the brain, researchers are now suggesting that when your body is relaxed and your mind is calm, the analytical left hemisphere seems to be more closely in touch with the visual right hemisphere. In fact, the level of calmness, or frequency of brain waves, appears to be a very important factor in brain inter-hemispheric communication.

Brain-wave patterns are labeled in four basic categories depending on the number or cycles per second. The most active state, *beta* (14-30 hertz [Hz], or cycles per second), occurs when we are anxiously concentrating on a task, or when we feel anxiety or fear. In the next mental state, *alpha* (8-13Hz), we are awake and alert, yet tranquil, serene and relaxed. Researchers have found that in the alpha state we are more receptive to ideas. This means we are more receptive to spiritual promptings to our individual spirit, and more receptive to commands from our spirit to our mortal intellect. The last two stages are *theta* (4-7 Hz) and *delta* (1.5-.5 Hz) ranging respectively from deep reverie through sleep and into deep, dreamless sleep.

Knowing how to leave beta and spend a few minutes in alpha enable us to take a pleasant, refreshing break during an otherwise hectic day. Learning to relax in this manner not only helps us to cope with the remainder of a busy day, but relaxation periods are proving to be an alternative to drugs in the treatment of ulcers, headaches, insomnia, etc.

Alpha, therefore, is the ideal and recommended mental state for focusing the Eye of Faith. In the routine of our lives, of course, this is not always possible. The responsibilities and pressures of daily living often make this a difficult state to achieve. We must always remember, the Eye of Faith may be focused at any time, even in the midst of hassled frustration and pressure, if our intent is real for a righteous purpose. Be aware, however, agitation blocks the spirit.

". . . they had beheld with an eye of faith, and they were glad."
(Ether 12:19)

5

ACKNOWLEDGING THE POWER OF THE EYE OF FAITH

Although in the Lord's infinite wisdom unto Him "all things are spiritual" (D&C 29:34), in our mortal finite perspective we experience a wide range of endeavors.

Eye of Faith IN EVERY REALM OF ENDEAVOR

The Eye of Faith may be illuminated and focused in every aspect of our lives, in every realm of endeavor:

- **The Spiritual Realm**

This is the all-encompassing realm, permeating through the others, in which we become more focused in prayer, more unconditional in love, more receptive to the Holy Ghost, more responsive to inspiration and more worthy in ministering to others, etc.

- **The Therapeutic Realm**

This is the making-things-right realm in which we are teaching, encouraging, helping, healing, correcting, blessing and inspiring, etc.

- **The Affectionate Realm**

   This is the caring-for-others realm in which we are experiencing concern, affection, love, devotion and responsibility for others, etc.

- **The Triumphant Realm**

   This is the winning-succeeding realm in which we are striving to make a living, earn good grades, accomplish tasks, overcome weaknesses and achieve goals, etc.

- **The Aesthetic Realm**

   This is the creative-artistic realm in which we are enjoying music, experiencing beauty in art, dance, nature and everyday living, etc.

- **The Well-Being Realm**

   This is the amelioration realm in which we enhance our usefulness, strengthen our physical stamina, nourish ourselves wisely, maintain emotional stability and enrich our relationships, etc.

- **A Combination of Realms**

   Although at any given moment one realm or another may emerge as the most crucial, our endeavors usually comprise a combination of two or more realms at the same time. Likewise, every endeavor in every realm of our lives transpires on a continuum between what may be termed temporal at one extreme and spiritual at another.

Eye of Faith = TEMPORAL and SPIRITUAL POWER

Although the Lord said that unto Him "all things are spiritual" (D&C 29:34), there are endeavors in our lives we consider to be more temporal than spiritual.

Most of our efforts to exercise faith will be dependent upon divine power far beyond our own. However, to honor our agency and provide for our development and progression, the Lord intends for us to make some decisions on our own, and has made it clear that it is not appropriate for us to be commanded by Him in all the affairs of our lives (see D&C 58:26).

We should apply ourselves in all diligence without expecting a revelation on every decision and responsibility. However, we should constantly counsel with Him (see D&C 58:25).

On a number of occasions, even during those critical years when the Church was in its latter-day infancy, the saints were instructed to use their own judgment in some matters. In several responses to inquiries, the Lord responded: "It mattereth not unto me" (D&C 60:5, 61:22, 62:5).

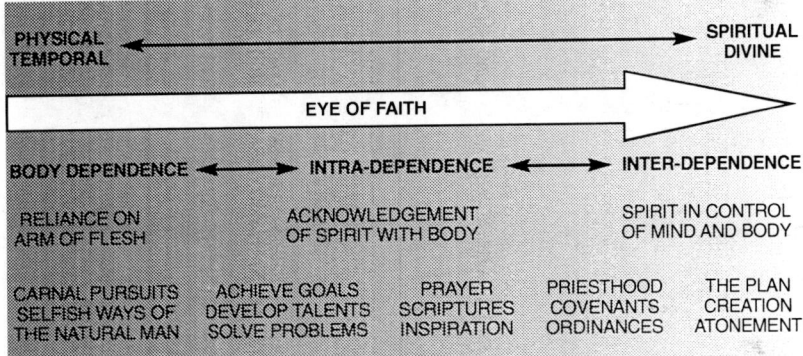

Illustration 27

At one extreme of the continuum is total dependence on the natural man, an enemy to God. At the other extreme of the continuum is our total dependence upon divine power beyond our own, "For we know that it is by grace that we are saved, after all we can do" (2 Nephi 25:23).

Eye of Faith and INTRA-DEPENDENCE

Intra-dependence occurs within ourselves as the body and the spirit depend upon one another. As we learn to focus our Eye of

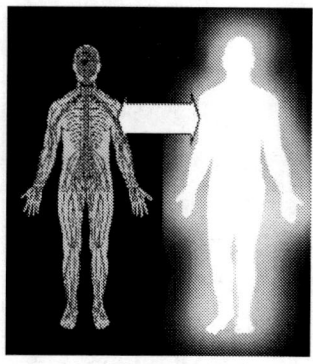

Illustration 28

Faith and enhance communication between our divine spirit and our mortal intellect, we increase command of the spirit over the body, and thus advance on the continuum. Many personal objectives of a more temporal nature may be the focal point of the Eye of Faith in this range of the continuum. The intra-dependent aspects of our lives, as we learn to place the spirit in command over the body, are extremely important phases in our eternal development.

Indeed, the agency of personal choice our Savior so valiantly defended in the pre-mortal realm of the courts on high has far more effect and is far more under our personal control than many realize.

As we exercise our agency in righteousness, we soon recognize the wide latitude of choice before us. Faith in ourselves and a degree of independence is important and appropriate in our efforts to become more self-sufficient. However, faith in ourselves is justified only by virtue of our obedience to divine principles and an awareness of our dependency upon divine direction and assistance. We must always remember our dependency, "For we know that it is by grace that we are saved, after all we can do" (2 Nephi 25:23).

Eye of Faith and INTER-DEPENDENCE

Inter-dependence occurs between ourselves and the Holy Ghost, our Savior and our Father in Heaven. This is why the "Essential Foundation "s in Chapter 3 are so vital. Most of our growth and development, and our preparation for eternal life, will occur in an inter-dependent relationship with the Holy Ghost, our Savior and our Father in Heaven.

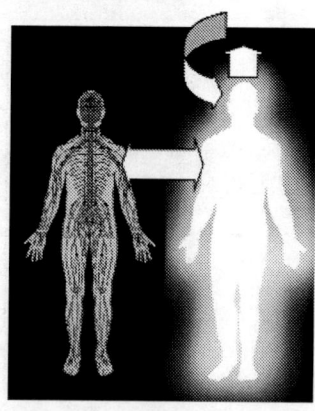

Illustration 29

Whether the endeavor be temporal or spiritual, the Eye of Faith is the most powerful, natural and lasting way to achieve results in the full spectrum of our daily lives . . .

from:	to:
children to guide	teenagers to discipline
standards to uphold	goals to achieve
addictions to defeat	relationships to improve
decisions to make	challenges to face
lessons to prepare	talks to deliver
habits to break	testimonies to strengthen
callings to magnify	blessings to pronounce
attributes to recognize	confidences to build
temptations to resist	fears to vanquish
handicaps to overcome	weaknesses to replace
trespasses to forgive	trials to endure well

Eye of Faith in THREE TEMPORAL EXAMPLES

Although I have witnessed remarkable results and numerous testimonies of the power of the Eye of Faith in sacred matters such as marriage and family relationships, pronouncing blessings and other spiritual endeavors, I consider them too sacred and too confidential to describe herein. The following are three examples of a more temporal nature.

- **Eye of Faith and DIVING THE DIVE**

A mother in our neighborhood called me in despair one day and asked if I would have time to help her 17-year-old son who was failing in high school and she was afraid he would not graduate. She said he would not bring his textbooks home from school and hated to read.

I made an appointment to meet with the two of them in their home. This occurred during the summer between the boy's junior and senior year. I will call him Jim. As we sat down together in their living room, I asked Jim what was most important to him at that time in his life. He said it was to be able to perform a particularly difficult dive in competition. I told him to put on his swimming suit and meet us at their back yard swimming pool.

I chose to introduce Jim first to a few principles of the Eye of Faith illuminants to focus upon an objective most meaningful to him at that moment. I knew that once he had confidence in what I would later ask him to do, he would willingly focus his Eye of Faith upon academic achievement.

When Jim arrived at the pool, I told him to step onto the diving board and describe in detail the dive he was having so much trouble mastering. He walked to the edge of the board, told me how many times and how high he was to jump, how his feet were to land on the board, the balance and shifting of his weight, at what point in the air he was to bend and spin, etc. After he described the dive in words only, I said let's go back inside.

I explained the nature of the Eye of Faith in general and emphasized a few relevant illuminants. To help him understand the significance of specific details and genuine feelings, I mentally walked him through a visual example. I told him to close his eyes and envision and feel every motion and sensation I described. I took him through every phase of his dive, including his emotional state and feelings of touch. For example, it was important that he actually feel the rough texture of the diving board under his bare feet as he approached his dive. After fewer than five minutes, I said, "let's go back out to the pool . . . I want to see that dive."

As his mother and I looked on, Jim confidently took his position on the diving board and, with no hesitation, sailed into the air. Before he came up out of the water his mother exclaimed, loud enough for the neighbors to hear, "He's never been able to do that before!" Jim's head surfaced and he literally yelled with joy. I said, "put your clothes on, young man, we've some important things to talk about." I knew I had his complete trust. When he came back into the living room with his hair still wet, my first challenge was to calm him down from his excitement.

Because he did so well, I knew Jim had the innate conceptualization skills he would need to do what I was going to ask him to do to improve his academic performance. In my experience I have discovered that many people, although they may be intelligent and educated, are really unable to envision properly. This is one reason why the previous chapter on "Correcting Impaired Vision of the Eye of Faith" is so important.

I then asked Jim which of all his textbooks he disliked the most. He quickly said chemistry and history. I at this time described the significance of each dynamic of the Eye of Faith. In his prayers, among other things, he was to experience a genuine desire to learn, to envision the pages of those textbooks and anticipate that the information thereon may someday help him to solve problems and achieve goals.

Jim became an excellent student during his senior year. I can still remember him asking me for permission to use these principles when he went on his mission. He saw them as a way to help people overcome addictions in order to observe the Word of Wisdom. Jim served a successful mission and often stops by my office to keep me abreast of things happening in the lives of his wife and children.

- **Eye of Faith IN A JALOPY CONVERTIBLE**

A talented young man who fit the popular description of tall, dark and handsome, moved into our ward with his family while he was Priest age. I will call him Bob. A year later he enrolled in several college courses I was teaching, just about one semester before he would be called to serve a full-time mission for the Church.

From several courses, I formed a broadcasting organization of news writers, producers, announcers, videographers, studio camera operators, etc. The students were to select their own leaders such as production managers, program directors, station managers and one general manager to be over everything.

Bob was elevated to that top position with about 85 students under his supervision. Although he was capable and confident, he came to my office late one afternoon and said things were falling apart between himself and his family and wanted to know if I could help him.

Although our ward was divided in the meantime and Bob was now in a different ward, he knew I was well acquainted with his parents, so he described the situation in detail.

Bob's real mother had passed away, and his father had remarried a lovely, active member of the Church. Bob said she was wonderful, and he knew she was right, but they always quarreled whenever it was his turn to do the dishes.

He said the chores had been fairly and equally distributed among family members, and Tuesday nights were his turn to do the dishes.

This conversation took place on one of those Tuesdays, and he said he just couldn't stand the thought of going home that night. He explained that he always arrived home late on Tuesdays and after he ate he was to clear the table and do the dishes.

Bob told me that he knew this was a fair assignment and his stepmother had every right to get after him, but he just couldn't stand going home to the dirty dishes and doing them.

I described to Bob the principles of the Eye of Faith and emphasized the relevant illuminants he was to observe when he arrived home that evening. I told him to park his little jalopy convertible as he always did in front of his home. Tonight, however, he was to remain in the car and engage in a prayer unlike any he had ever offered.

Among other things, he was to experience himself walking up the walkway to his home, feel the doorknob in his hand and step into his living room feeling happy and grateful he had a family living there who loved him . . . who left well-prepared and balanced meals for him to eat by just sitting down at the table . . . to really feel happiness to the point of whistling a tune . . . to really feel genuine gratitude . . . to realize that doing the dishes once a week was his opportunity to show his love and appreciation to his family . . . to experience himself actually clearing the table and doing the dishes with that same feeling of happiness and gratitude. In other words, he was to focus his Eye of Faith in compliance with the laws upon which the blessings he sought were predicated.

The next morning between classes Bob came to my office and excitedly said he had to talk to me. As this strong and confident young man sat down, tears welled up in his eyes and he said, "Brother McIntyre, you won't believe what happened last night."

When I got out of the car, after doing what you had asked me to do, I thought 'Oh, I'll probably just try harder to get along tonight, but I don't feel any different. But, as I stepped into the living room I broke into a whistle. I never whistle. I stopped right there and stood in the middle of the room, shocked that I was whistling. I then realized I did feel completely different. I know you've got to hurry to your next class. To make a long story short, I'll just tell you that Mom and I joked and laughed together all the way through the dishes. It was wonderful. I'll never dread doing those dishes again."

The next day he filled in the details and told me all that had happened. This young man truly focused his Eye of Faith. He patiently sat in his car and faithfully did everything I had asked him to do. He felt the doorknob in his hand and tried to literally experience and believe what he thought would be impossible. He successfully delivered a command from his divine spirit to his mortal brain, which is totally obedient to the spirit, and to which his mortal body responded.

Bob was soon called to serve his mission in France where I served, so he wrote to me in French and told me how he was teaching the principles to investigators to help them overcome Word of Wisdom problems. This young man is a successful attorney today and, no doubt, still focusing his Eye of Faith.

- **Eye of Faith and GRADES IN COLLEGE**

One day after a class I was teaching at a community college, one of my students, a middle-aged woman I will call Ann, came to me and said she had heard of the help I had given other students.

She asked if I would consider helping her because her husband was upset with her for trying to go to school at this stage in her life and wanted her to quit. She said she was only taking one other class, but because she had failed the last two tests, her husband was all the more convinced she was wasting time and money.

Ann said she desperately wanted an education and felt that her husband would be more understanding if she were doing better in her computer course, which she was failing at this time. She explained that she read the chapters many times and studied very hard before the tests. But, she said, her mind always went blank during the test. She said she was sure she knew the material, but just couldn't think clearly during the tests.

Ann also told me that she felt that the other students didn't like her and wondered why such an "old lady" would take such a class. I asked her if anyone had ever said anything to make her feel that way. She answered no; she just felt that way.

Ann was especially stressed as we talked because her third test was scheduled for the following morning. I outlined for her the illuminants of the Eye of Faith and detailed a few examples of what should be included in her petition, such as genuinely feeling that the younger students probably admired her for wanting to improve her knowledge and skills and, among other things, to trust in the reality that she had prepared well, and to envision a confident and calm countenance, even a smile on her lips. She said she would put her heart and soul into it.

Ann came early to my classroom two days later and joyously told me what happened. She said she parked her car and walked across campus to the place for her test. As she walked, she felt her effort was in vain because she became increasingly frightened and felt that she would fail the test again. "But," she said, "as I walked through the door of the classroom a sudden rush of tranquility came over me. I felt calm and found myself saying to myself, 'I'm really glad the test is today. I feel ready to take it.' She also said she was the first one in the room and that as other students came into the room they greeted her and made comments about the exam.

She said she felt she was one of them, and just felt like kidding with them. As Ann took the test, she realized she was doing well and was one of the first ones to finish. As she walked out of the room, and handed her completed test to the professor at the door, she told him this was the easiest one so far. He replied, "Funny you would say that, this third test is the one the students complain about the most."

That's all Ann knew when she talked to me, but she couldn't wait to find out her score which would be posted the following class period.

Two days later Ann rushed into my office to let me know she missed an 'A' by only a few points. What excited her the most was that a girl sitting by her, who received 'A's on her first two tests, received only a 'C' on this third test. It was, indeed, more difficult. Ann earned "A's on all the remaining tests and received a final grade of 'A' for the course.

It should be noted that when Ann focused her Eye of Faith that first time, she focused only upon her conduct in the classroom. This explains why she still felt fear as she walked across the campus.

Ann's husband became supportive of her returning to school, and she thanked me all semester long. It was not me she should thank, however, but a wise Creator who endowed even our mortal bodies with enormous capacity for growth and improvement when the spirit is in command.

Eye of Faith AND UPLIFTING OTHERS

By righteously awakening, brightly illuminating and clearly focusing the Eye of Faith, we may influence for good the lives of others more powerfully and more lastingly than by following all the strategies devised by man. The subtle yet powerful micromomentary expressions described in Chapter 4, and the personal radiance described by President McKay above and more thoroughly in a later section (see pp. 145-147), are examples of the magnitude of ways the Eye of Faith may enable us to uplift others.

When we focus the Eye of Faith upon ※s in which we see dormant potential flourish, those marvelous micromomentary expressions genuinely appear and, although unseen by mortal eyes, penetrate, lift, encourage and inspire with remarkable results.

The incomparable Eye of Faith may see invisible potential and dormant but praiseworthy qualities in all of us, unseen by mortal eyes, and to which we would otherwise be oblivious. Powerful ※s transform wishful thinking beyond even a brightness of hope into levels of personal expression and radiance that literally inspire others into improvement and progression.

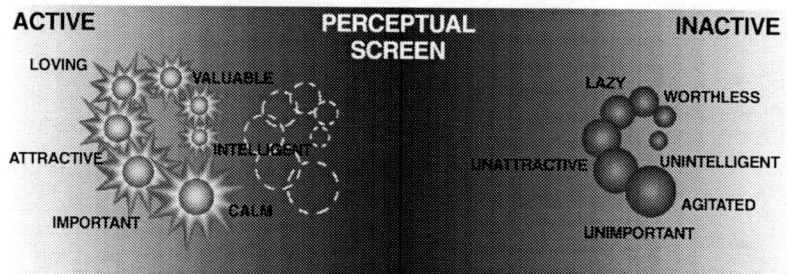

Illustration 30

Eye of Faith AND OUR CONVICTIONS

We are told numerous times in both ancient and latter-day scripture that we must be in a believing state of mind to receive the blessing. However, belief cannot be forced. We either do or we don't. Belief must come naturally and genuinely. So, where do we start? How do we strengthen a conviction?

Although beliefs, attitudes, and values cannot be seen directly, we all know they exist. They are very meaningful to us and may be observed in our actions and inferred from our emotions.

To differentiate between the three: our *beliefs* may be thought of as our view of things on a true-false continuum. Our *attitudes* may be characterized as our response to things on a positive-negative continuum, and our *values* are enduring concepts on a right-wrong continuum.

It is axiomatic that worthwhile endeavors produce desirable results. That is, if a seed is good (see Alma 32:28-42), it will produce good fruit. If a chemical formula is based upon true principles, it will cause the expected effect. If advice is sound and accurate, it will bring about whatever it promises.

In other words, the test of whether or not something is good or bad, true or false, worthwhile or worthless, etc., is the result it produces.

Perhaps someone older and wiser, or someone you respect, or even a Prophet of God has advised you to do something, or to avoid something. You would like to believe what they say, but you just can't seem to make yourself believe it to the point you will obey, although you really wish you could. This is an excellent opportunity for you to illuminate and focus your Eye of Faith.

In fact, if you have justifiable reason to want to place trust or confidence in a particular belief, and develop faith in a given principle, or an event, etc., there is no more powerful way to do this than to open your Eye of Faith and focus on an appropriate and relevant ☀.

The ☀ will depend upon the nature of the principle or event, etc. and your personal interpretation of its promise or fulfillment. This is one reason why becoming more and more familiar with the scriptures is so important. As much as possible, through your Eye of Faith, refine the belief to a specific event, see it in action, and see the blessing attained, the promise fulfilled.

By so doing, you may gain sufficient trust in the belief to put it to the test. This is to say, opening and appropriately focusing your Eye of Faith will help you acquire confidence in the belief to the extent that you will be able to comply with the conditions necessary to give the belief a fair chance. If the belief is founded upon true principles, you will eventually recognize its value and realize the fulfillment of its promises.

With your new or increased understanding of the Eye of Faith, read again Alma 32:27-43.

Eye of Faith, LEARNING AND REMEMBERING

In addition to spiritual growth and righteous results, when you meaningfully illuminate and purposefully focus your Eye of Faith you perform an intellectual process scientists have found to be healthy for the brain. Like muscles, the brain actually strengthens by increasing the number of blood vessels and the density of nerve connections. For example, focusing upon a scene requiring bodily motion stimulates the motor cortex portion of the brain, which controls muscle movement, causing minute movement in the involved muscles. It might be said that focusing the Eye of Faith puts the brain through a neural workout.

Chapter 4 describes the dual hemispheric characteristics of the brain. The left hemisphere performs the linear, sequential functions; while the right hemisphere is the center for the aesthetic, simultaneous functions. The left sees the separate parts of something, the right sees the big picture in perspective. When reading, for example, the left hemisphere reads the words, the right envisions the ideas.

More importantly, however, is the suggestion by neuroscientists that the ability to purposefully envision something dwells in the right hemisphere of the brain. The process of sharply focusing the Eye of Faith actually strengthens the functioning of the right hemisphere so essential in the expansion of our memories, the acquisition of knowledge and the development of originality and creativity.

Unfortunately, textbooks, classroom lectures and many other teaching-learning strategies develop primarily the left hemisphere only. We begin to think unnaturally in words.

In fact, one reason we read as slowly as we do is because we say the words to ourselves in our minds as we read. As you read this paragraph—if you listen carefully—you'll realize you're hearing yourself say the words in your mind as you read them. This is common with almost everyone, and it holds back our reading speed to the rate of spoken words and sentences.

Your mind, however, can receive and understand information many times faster than this. This is the reason why one of the most important elements in a speed reading course is the attempt to teach the student to read without saying the words in the mind. Once the reader breaks that habit, speed and comprehension begin to increase rapidly.

It seems to be that as we shift from reading words to envisioning the ideas the words symbolize, our comprehension is more natural and comfortable. We will also retain what we read much longer. This is one reason why memory experts stress so emphatically the need to visualize the numbers, objects, etc. their subjects are trying to memorize.

Educational psychologists and learning specialists suggest a holistic or total approach to learning in which both hemispheres of the brain are interactive via the corpus callosum, a small membrane connecting the two cerebral hemispheres (see Chapter 4). Whether a person is learning to speak a foreign language, improve basketball skills, or excel at any endeavor, mental processes should work in harmony with one another.

In addition to harmony, the two hemispheres should be more in balance. During the first few years of life we use both hemispheres about equally and they are of comparable strength. During those early years, we learn about 25 times more per day than we do as adults, after we use only the left side.

Researchers also suggest that what they refer to as the mind, or the origination of thought, dwells in the right hemisphere where creative ideas are formed. This suggests a key role for the right hemisphere in the vital relationship between the brain and the divine spirit, where thought actually originates.

Consequently, the more we illuminate and focus the Eye of Faith the healthier the brain will be, the more the right hemisphere will be strengthened, the more harmony will be improved and the more balance will be achieved between the two hemispheres, increasing our capacity to acquire and retain information.

Eye of Faith AND PERSONAL PRAYER

Although you may awaken and focus your Eye of Faith often for many purposes without engaging in formal prayer, you should always focus your Eye of Faith when you are praying. In other words, you may focus your Eye of Faith without praying, but you should never pray without focusing your Eye of Faith.

In fact, evidence that (1) the language of the mortal brain is ●, and (2) divine communication to mortal beings is symbolic to deliberately elicit ●s, and (3) the power of choice in thought origination dwells in the eternal spirit, not the mortal brain, and (4) it is the divine spirit that initiates original thought, not the mortal brain, and (5) the divine spirit should be in total and continual command of the mortal brain, to which the mortal body faithfully responds, and (6) we should pray "believing" we will receive, and (8) believing is in reality literally "seeing," elevates the process and power of awakening and focusing the Eye of Faith, while in prayer, to its highest level of significance during our mortal probation.

All of the Eye of Faith illuminants in Chapter 3 are important and will improve personal prayer, especially calmness, initiative and specificity.

Although we should be as calm as possible during personal prayer, we are often under stress and agitation when we are most in need of prayer. In fact, our frame of mind is often: 'I'm too upset to pray'. Usually, it is when we least feel like praying that our need to pray is the greatest. At other times, we are literally driven to our knees in total frustration, even despair.

Focusing the Eye of Faith during such times, under stress and extreme circumstances, is the most powerful way to gain composure. As we focus the Eye of Faith first upon one or more of the "Essential Foundation �," a peaceful serenity falls upon us and we gain both composure and control as much as possible, even in the face of discouragement, heart-ache, distress, loss and fear.

Centuries before Joseph Smith's birth, prophets knew he would be the human instrument through whom the Gospel would be restored to earth. However, and always remember: the First Vision occurred only after he went into the grove and sought divine guidance.

We must, therefore, take initiative and be specific in prayer. As you study the life of the Prophet Joseph, you will find that almost all significant doctrine came in response to his questions and requests for clarification.

The Prophet Joseph's experiences also offer us excellent examples of why we must be more specific in our prayers. We often over-generalize when we pray, rationalizing that Heavenly Father already knows the intents of our hearts. We are failing to comply with eternal law when we do this. We must be more specific and clearly know in our own minds the exact purposes for which we are praying.

Observing some or all of the Eye of Faith illuminants during prayer will help immensely to open channels of divine communication between spirit and spirit, and between your spirit and your mortal body. Therefore, when you pray, illuminate and focus your Eye of Faith upon scenes in which you envision.

HEAVENLY FATHER (see James E. Faust on pp. 51 & 60) and our SAVIOR as Mediator, the PERSON(S) for whom you are praying, the CONDITION(S) and CIRCUMSTANCE(S) for which you are praying, the RESULTS as though they were already achieved, and the BLESSINGS you are seeking, as though they were already granted. In other words, trust completely in the Lord, and clearly envision and wholeheartedly anticipate the righteous desires of your heart.

And when you are expressing GRATITUDE, be specific and literally envision, clearly and vividly, the events and circumstances for which you are thankful. When you express gratitude in this manner, you will be more sincere and you will avoid the mindless expressions of thanks we tend to say in the same words over and over again.

Finally, and always remember, you may focus your Eye of Faith anytime, anywhere, for whatever purpose you choose, in the form of a prayer in your heart.

Eye of Faith in SPEAKING and BLESSING

In the previous chapter you read of perception and inception, the interpretation of incoming messages, and the organizing of outgoing messages, respectively. Just as the myriad of ●s in the active domain control the interpretation of what we perceive, those same ●s form the control center of what we organize in order to form messages, whether written, spoken, gestured or otherwise. You may recall the examples of "pomme" and "pamplemousse" in Chapter 2, and especially the "Perceptual Views" and "Inceptual Responses" sections in Chapter 4.

The most effective way to supply the active domain with ●s conducive to spiritual power when speaking, teaching or pronouncing blessings, is to "treasure up in your minds continually the words of life" (D&C 84:85). As we do this we insert everlasting truths directly into the active domain. Although we may not be able to recall them, and we assume they are forgotten, they remain ready for the Holy Ghost to conjoin them to our spirit which encompasses the active domain, and it shall be given you when you need it: "For it shall be given you in the very hour, yea in the very moment, what ye shall say" (D&C 100:6).

With respect to fear when speaking before others, it is worthwhile to note that professional speakers, professors of speech and textbooks of human communication emphasize that one of the most effective ways to overcome fear and gain composure is to visualize oneself in the process of giving the speech, while appearing calm and confident, prior to speaking. Although the proponents of this procedure do not understand the relationship of the spirit to the body, this method is successful because they are unknowingly using one small phase of the Eye of Faith.

I have taught this method to many hundreds of students and have seen remarkable results. Even returned missionaries, with all their experience, are amazed at their increase in composure and assurance. I simply teach them to envision themselves in front of their audience or congregation as though they were seated in the congregation looking up at themselves. They are then to zoom in to a close-up view of their face and see a calm and pleasant expression. I also have them assume that they are actually in front of the congregation, seeing their audience before them, and feeling emotionally in control.

Inasmuch as speaking before others is ranked as the most frightening of all experiences, even more frightening than going to the dentist, many may benefit from this approach.

You can greatly improve upon the above method by using some or all of the Eye of Faith illuminants in Chapter 3.

When we bless children, seal anointings, pronounce blessings during confirmations, settings apart, ordinations, etc., we should literally see through the Eye of Faith and envision the actual conditions and circumstances we seek or pronounce. We should see them as though they were already granted, as did the righteous Jaredites who "saw with their eyes the things which they had beheld with an eye of faith."

In no other relationship will it be more important to do so than in our divine communication, for this relationship improves all others.

Eye of Faith AND DIVINE COMMUNICATION

Modern and ancient scripture makes it clear that divine communication, from inspiration to revelation, comes through the spirit personage of the Holy Ghost to our individual spirits. The Prophet Joseph Smith emphasized that this communication is from spirit to spirit when he said it occurs "precisely as though we had no bodies at all:" "All things whatsoever God in his infinite wisdom has seen fit and proper to reveal to us, while we are dwelling in mortality, in regard to our mortal bodies, are revealed to us in the abstract, and independent of affinity of this mortal tabernacle, but are revealed to our spirits precisely as though we had no bodies at all, and these revelations which will save our spirits will save our bodies."[1]

The content of the active domain determines the composition of the spiritual messages we are able to send, and the accessibility of those we hope to receive. When we purposefully open our Eye of Faith and generate a righteous ☀, we not only thrust out of the active domain any opposing ●, we also initiate multi-directional communication that opens the way for our righteous intent to be fully realized.

The frequencies transmitted by radio and television stations are surrounding us continually, from all around the world, yet are only detectable with a radio or television set tuned to a specific frequency. In a similar manner, divine communication is available to us at any given moment. However, a man-made apparatus, no matter how advanced it may be, is unable to engage in spiritual communication. Divine communication occurs only between spirit and spirit, and only when divine laws are obeyed.

It is very important to realize and always remember: your righteous experiences, no matter how long ago they occurred, and the truths you learn as you "treasure up in your minds continually the words of life, . . . shall be given you in the very hour . . ." (D&C 84:85). In other words, the Holy Ghost may retrieve from your active domain any righteous ●s you worthily placed therein, whether or not you remember doing so, and bring them to your remembrance, and facilitate your ability to express them at the right times and in appropriate circumstances for righteous purposes.

---

[1] *Scriptural Teachings of the Prophet Joseph Smith,* p. 398.

Thus we see, divine communication may occur in all directions: (1) upward and downward figuratively, or in other words, to your own spirit and from your own spirit in communication that includes prayer, expressions of gratitude, pleas for blessings, promptings of the Holy Ghost and revelation, (2) internally within when you take initiative and place your own divine spirit in direct command over the silent internal synapses between your cerebral neurons which control your mortal intellect and thus your mortal behavior, and (3) outward sideways figuratively in ways that may explain why we feel differently in different circumstances and in the presence of different people, and why there is mounting evidence that we actually effect and even create many of the circumstances and opportunities in our lives. The choice is in the domain of each and every one of our personal spirits with abilitating and facilitating ☀s or debilitating and limiting ●s.

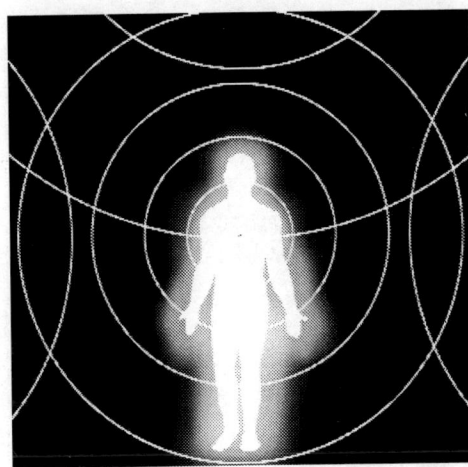

Illustration 31

Faith at times appears to be an illusive, vague and fleeting principle, difficult to exercise. Righteously focusing your Eye of Faith enables you to advance from wishful thinking to taking initiative by placing your own divine spirit in direct command over the silent internal synapses between your cerebral neurons. You thereby control the "natural man" and enhance your levels of spiritual power and usefulness to others.

REALITY of RADIANCE : RADIANCE of REALITY

Everything is composed of matter, including spirit. As the Lord revealed in the Doctrine and Covenants,

> There is no such thing as immaterial matter. All spirit is matter, but it is more fine or pure, and can only be discerned by purer eyes; We cannot see it; but when our bodies are purified we shall see that it is all matter (D&C 131:7-8).

The following eight sections are devoted to the reality or actuality of divine radiance prevailing in our daily lives, and the radiance of reality or truth permeating through all of creation to guide us back to the presence of heavenly parents.

Eye of Faith and THE LIGHT OF CHRIST

Our Redeemer identified himself as "the light and the life of the world" (D&C 12:9). This declaration is far more than a figurative phrase and should not be viewed as mere symbolism. Keep in mind the fact that everything, including spirit, is matter as you read the following of ". . . truth, and whatsoever is truth is light, and whatsoever is light is Spirit" (D&C 84:45), and we know: "all spirit is matter" (D&C 131:8).

> This is the light of Christ. As also he is in the sun, and the light of the sun, and the power thereof by which it was made. As also he is in the moon, and is the light of the moon, and the power thereof by which it was made; as also the light of the stars, and the power thereof by which they were made; and the earth also, and the power thereof, even the earth upon which you stand. And the light which shineth, which giveth you light, is through him who enlighteneth your eyes, which is the same light that quickeneth your understandings; which light proceedeth forth from the presence of God to fill the immensity of space—the light which is in all things, which giveth life to all things, which is the law by which all things are governed (D&C 88:7-13).

This marvelous realization, though impossible for us to fully comprehend, helps us understand that He not only serves as our perfect example as He lived on earth during the meridian of time, and also as our divine Redeemer who wrought the infinite atonement opening the way to immortality and eternal life, but long before and hereafter serves as our source of all light, all life and all truth (see Ether 4:12; Mosiah 16:9; D&C 10:70; 45:7; 50:24, 27).

Furthermore, this same "light" the scriptures call the Light of Christ is placed within the spirit of everyone who is born into this world (D&C 84:46; 93:2; Moroni 7:16; John 1:9) as the source of reason and conscience. The Light of Christ persuades men to do good and enables them to discern between good and evil (Moroni 7:16-18).

When a person willingly accepts this guiding influence, and hearkens to its soft promptings, relevant ●s are quickened, improving perceptions of truth and clarifying distinctions between good and evil. As some ●s are placed in perspective, and others relegated to the inactive domain, the person will be led to higher levels of spiritual conduct and what may be termed the higher light of the Holy Ghost.

Eye of Faith and the POWER OF THE HOLY GHOST

As the third member of the Godhead, unlike the Father and the Son, the Holy Ghost "is a personage of Spirit. Were it not so, the Holy Ghost could not dwell in us" (D&C 132:22).

The Holy Ghost is a man, a distinct entity. He does not transform himself into any other form, and he is only in one place at a time. However, his power and influence is manifest through all the immensity of time and space.

Because he is a "personage of spirit," he has the unique power within the eternal laws to literally radiate information, comprehension, accurate perception, all in absolute truth to our mortal intellects as the messenger of the Father and the Son.

It is important to distinguish between the Power of the Holy Ghost and the Gift of the Holy Ghost. The Power of the Holy Ghost radiates a temporary witness, whereas the Gift of the Holy Ghost is a permanent companionship. The Gift of the Holy Ghost will be treated in the following section.

All truth, all discoveries of truth, whether in a test tube or an electrical circuit, come to our attention as mortal beings through the Holy Ghost. This is a radiant transaction from spirit to spirit. Insights, warnings and all other wonderful messages from the Holy Ghost "are revealed to our spirits precisely as though we had no bodies at all."[2]

In addition to radiating information and knowledge, the Holy Ghost witnesses that what he radiates is indeed true. When we speak by the power of the Holy Ghost, a witness of what we say (a spiritual conviction of its truthfulness) is radiated directly to the spirit of the person or persons to whom we are speaking.

Thus we see, the Power of the Holy Ghost is two-fold: He is the radiant means by which we receive the message, and He radiates a confirmation of the validity of the message.

Through the miraculous nature of His power, the Holy Ghost radiates spontaneous personal messages, promptings that may occur in a fraction of a second, a sudden impulse to do something, or to avoid something.

In other instances, His radiance may simultaneously enable many in a congregation to receive personal insight, different from the others, although from the same words and by the same speaker.

On a universal scale, in a complex sophistication of communication we do not understand, His radiance may be received by an infinite number of us, anywhere on earth, at any time of day or night, both spontaneously and simultaneously.

Prior to baptism, the radiant influences of the Power of the Holy Ghost, although marvelous in scope and manifestation, are only temporary.

---

[2] *Scriptural Teachings of the Prophet Joseph Smith*, p. 398 (see Chapter 3).

Eye of Faith and the GIFT OF THE HOLY GHOST

After baptism, we are entitled to receive the Gift of the Holy Ghost, a constant companion, a permanent influence, the greatest gift we may receive during our mortal lives, so long as we remain worthy.

A model example of the relationship between the Power of the Holy Ghost and the Gift of the Holy Ghost occurred in a dramatic experience I had just after I arrived in Switzerland as a missionary to serve as the President of the Geneva Branch of the Church. I discovered that a non-member husband of a life-long member of the Church had been meeting with different pairs of missionaries on a weekly basis for several years. Some members said he had been meeting with missionaries for more than 10 years.

He was a talented and handsome man who earned his living as a professional piano player. He obeyed the Word of Wisdom, attended Sacrament Meeting regularly and lived the tenants of the Gospel. However, he refused to be baptized.

I arranged for my companion and me to begin meeting with him. Knowing that he was living his life just as though he were a member of the Church, I asked him why he had never accepted baptism.

He explained that the man he most admired was his deceased father, and that he felt he would betray his father if he left his father's church. He said that when the missionaries were in his home, whether Elders or sisters, he felt that what they were saying was true. However, within a few days, doubts would always arise. This pattern had been repeating every week for years.

I explained the difference between a temporary witness and the constant companionship of the Holy Ghost, and I then began to say things I did not realize I was saying: I promised him that once he was baptized and received the Gift of the Holy Ghost, he would never doubt the truthfulness of the Church again.

He agreed to be baptized. His wife, who was baptized at eight years of age, began to sob, then he began to weep. We set a date for his baptism and left. As we walked to our bicycles, my junior companion asked if I realized what I had said, and reminded me that I had promised this man that he would never doubt the Church again.

Now the full impact of what had taken place struck me with momentary fear. How could I have made such a promise? I quickly realized, however, that the promise did not come from me, but through me, and the next day we made arrangements for the baptism.

They were sealed in the Swiss Temple one year later. I receive a Christmas card every year and, for more than 30 years until his passing, each one confirmed the remarkable fact that not once did a doubt ever arise again.

This example demonstrates the importance and permanence of the Gift of the Holy Ghost beyond His temporary witness. In this case, the husband was worthy and prepared, so the time had arrived and the Holy Ghost literally took over.

This brother's relevant ●s were in harmony with the temporary witness he felt each time the missionaries bore testimony. However, "a man may receive the Holy Ghost, and it may descend upon him, and not tarry with him" (D&C 130:23). In the absence of the Gift of the Holy Ghost as a constant companion, which he could not receive until after baptism, the ●s in his active domain continued to dominate. Once he was baptized and received the Gift of the Holy Ghost by the laying on of hands by one having authority, the ●s that had caused his doubt were thrust into the inactive domain. He could recall the old thoughts, but their influence upon his feelings and behavior had vanished.

Eye of Faith and INFRASTRUCTURES OF MATTER

Just as "we shall see that it is all matter" (D&C 131:7-8), and just as our earth was created by organizing unorganized matter, so do all things have their form, substance and function according to their organizational infrastructure of matter. Our universe, for example, is a result of its infrastructure: the matter from which the planets, stars, etc. are composed and organized.

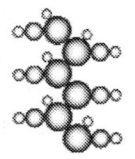

Illustration 32

Our earth, as a portion of the infrastructure of the universe, has its own infrastructure: the elements of which it is composed and organized. The rocks and soils of the earth all have their respective infrastructures, as do trees and other plants. Illustration 32 shows the molecular infrastructure of cellulose in a form of wood.

Illustration 33

Our mortal bodies are no exception, and are what they are because of their minute infrastructure: the tiny but powerful little cell that has its own infrastructure: the DNA helix, made up of chromosomes, which are made up of genes, which are made up of molecules, made up of atoms, with nuclei and protons, etc.

Just as it is the composition of the infrastructure that determines the characteristics of the physical world, including our mortal bodies, so is the very inception of an idea and the initiation of a thought the result of an infrastructure, the most important infrastructure of all: each and every ◯ and ⬤ in our active domains. After all, this is the infrastructure that will remain with us in "a perfect remembrance" (Alma 5:18) and traverse the veil with us when we pass from mortality into immortal realms. Once again, there is no more powerful and everlasting way to improve this all-important infrastructure than to replace useless and detrimental components with bright and powerful ✸s by illuminating and focusing the Eye of Faith.

Eye of Faith and ELECTROMAGNETIC ENERGY

Even invisible space is permeated with matter, and the space around us is vibrating as energy waves, including electromagnetic frequencies.

All radio and television programs ride through the electromagnetic spectrum invisible to our mortal eyes but totally and continually surrounding us wherever we may be. Were our ears able to hear, and our eyes able to see all the frequencies, we would pass out from pain or sensory overload.

As explained in more detail in Chapter 4, our mortal perception is a result of wisely placed physiological limitations over which we have little or no control. For example, we know that human eyes perceive only certain rays of the color spectrum because we are unable to see beyond the infrared and ultraviolet extremes at each end. Likewise, human ears are limited to a frequency range between 20 and 20,000 cycles per second. However, we know there are far more frequencies that are silent or invisible to us, as shown in Illustration 34.

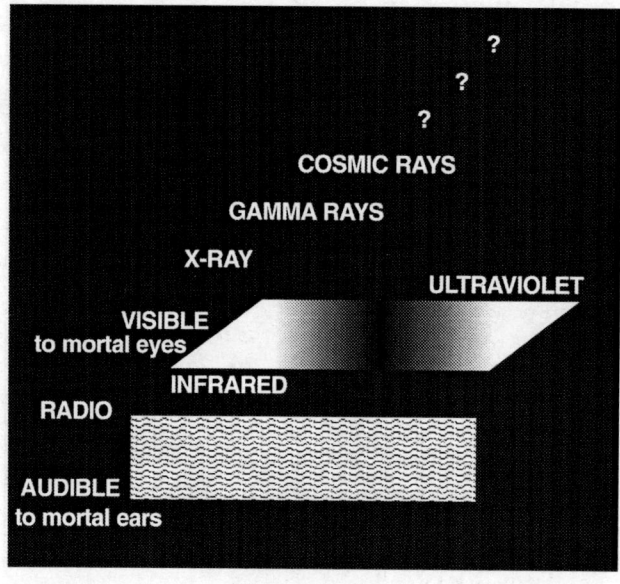

Illustration 34

A radio station transmits silent invisible electromagnetic signals that a radio's speakers convert to a frequency range that literally moves air molecules so they strike the tympanic membrane or eardrum in our ears, enabling us to hear the sound. In a similar manner, other frequencies are converted by our television sets into that portion of the spectrum we are able to see as well as hear.

Although only a very small portion of them are visible to our mortal eyes, there are many unseen but measurable frequencies of energy. It has not been revealed to us how the Holy Ghost fills the immensity of space with His influence. However, we may liken this power, unique in the Godhead, to transmission and reception forces we do understand.

For example, many broadcast stations are designated as directional so their signals or programming radiates out only in limited directions, usually two directions, instead of in a circumference. It has been known for some time that the transmission of radiating power may be impeded, even completely nullified. Likewise, and of far more significance to our personal and future lives, our sensitivity to the Light of Christ and our receptivity of the Holy Ghost may be impeded or even completely nullified, by disobedience.

Illustration 35

Eye of Faith: ATTRACTING and PROPELLING POWER

Each and every ⬤ and ⬤ is striving to fulfill its intent or purpose by attracting congruous or compatible ones (whether good or bad) and repelling incongruous, incompatible or opposing ones (whether good or bad). The emission and reception of energy forms at varying frequencies and intensities results in electro-chemical impulses in the mortal brain.

Our ⬤s in the active domain, in a marvelous electro-chemical relationship between the divine spirit and the mortal brain, are able to tune in to or receive incoming stimuli and emit outgoing stimuli. However, those ⬤s are only able to receive from and transmit to ⬤s mutually in phase or in harmony with one another. In like manner, the ⬤s will attract ⬤s that are congruous or compatible with ⬤s already in the active domain. You may recall from Chapter 2 that Brigham Young said: "The spirit is influenced by the body, and the body by the spirit."[3]

I return your attention to the jellybean story on the first page of the first chapter. You will recall that the colors of the different flavors appeared to change in intensity or vibrancy according to one's desire and expectation.

The members of the congregation wanted to confirm to themselves that they were not color blind and expected to see the respective colors more numerous according to my descriptions; demonstrating the inherent power we each have to draw from the circumstances in which we find ourselves at any given moment those features, attributes and conditions we genuinely want to see.

Many years later, my wife and I attended a sacrament meeting in a nearby stake because our oldest daughter and her husband were assigned to speak there. We were not told the subject of our daughter's talk. We arrived late, so we sat near the rear of the chapel.

To our surprise, our daughter spoke about the jellybean principle. When she showed the congregation a poster card only about one-third the size of the one I used originally, I thought to myself that it would be too small to be effective beyond the first few rows. I was amazed when an elderly couple sitting directly behind us on the back row began to whisper and he said, "I'm sure she really has several

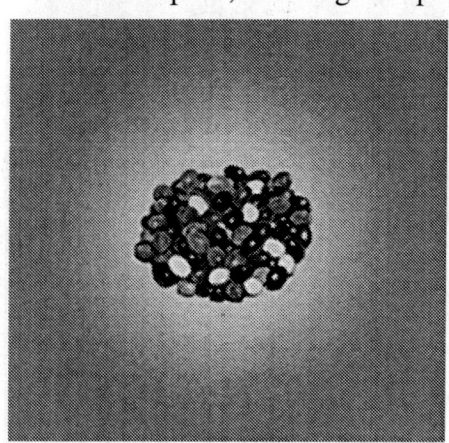
Illustration 36

---

[3] *Discourses of Brigham Young,* pp. 69-70.

cards up there." My wife heard his comment also, so we just smiled at each other.

Actually, color as we know it exists only in our internal visual system, not in nature. The objects in our lives have no known color, nor does color exist in the frequencies we receive as light reflecting from the objects. Without being too technical, each eye contains millions of light-sensitive cells known as photoreceptors. Light waves reflected from objects stimulate our photoreceptors, which in turn respond to the varying wavelengths of light by converting different frequencies into the perceptual colors of red, blue and green. Then, further into the system, neurons along the visual path mix and match until we perceive a full spectrum of the millions of color variations we perceive in our mortal world.

Eye of Faith and OUR PERSONAL RADIANCE

What is so remarkable about this attracting and repelling process is evidence that our ●s and ●s may reach out and attract from considerable distances, and transmit or emit out to affect or influence circumstances beyond our immediate presence or what we would assume to be our scope of influence. We broadcast our intention and invite in, or literally attract or draw in, available resources to realize or implement the intent, whether good or bad, right or wrong.

Speaking of personal radiance and the influence we may have upon one another, President David O. McKay said in a general conference:

> There is another responsibility correlated and even coexistent with free agency, which is too infrequently emphasized, and that is the effect not only of a person's actions but also of his thoughts upon others. Man radiates what he is, and that radiation affects to a greater or less degree every person who comes within that radiation."[4]

---

[4] President David O. McKay, General Conference Reports, April, 1950, p. 32; also in *Gospel Ideals,* Book IV, Chapter 22.

Years later, President McKay said:

> Into the hands of every individual is given a marvelous power for good or for evil, the silent, unconscious, unseen influence of his life. This is simply the constant radiation of what a man really is, not what he pretends to be. Every man, by his mere living, is radiating sympathy, or sorrow, or morbidness, or cynicism, or happiness, or hope, or any of a hundred other qualities. Life is a state of constant radiation and absorption; to exist is to radiate; to exist is to be the recipient of radiations.

Man cannot escape for one moment from this radiation of his character, this constantly weakening or strengthening of others. He cannot evade the responsibility by saying it is an unconscious influence. He can select the qualities that he will permit to be radiated. He can cultivate sweetness, calmness, trust, generosity, truth, justice, loyalty, nobility—make them vitally active in his character—and by these qualities he will constantly affect the world"[5]

A book entitled *Some Suggestions for Latter-day Saint Missionaries* was recommended reading by President David O. McKay when I went on my mission. One section of the book was about the visible human aura, colors radiating from the body that change in hue according to one's mood and extend varying distances from the body according to the intensity of one's emotion. The book explains that when the emotion of one person becomes strong enough, a corresponding effect and color occurs with someone in close proximity. Since that time, investigators have examined the visible aura with more sophisticated equipment and are using a special form of photography for therapeutic purposes.

Thus we see examples of how ◯s and ●s in the active domain influence the reception and interpretation of incoming external frequencies, and how ◯s and ●s in the active domain exert an external influence on other active domains. In the first instance, with the jellybean phenomenon, the colors did not change in intensity or vibrancy, nor did the light waves reflecting from the

---

[5] David O. McKay, *Man May Know For Himself,* p. 266.

jellybeans change in any manner. The reaction occurred internally, in the active domains, as ⬤s were introduced to the congregation in such a manner that the internal ⬤s or frequencies were in alignment or in phase with the external light waves to which the visual system was responding.

Eye of Faith SEES RADIANT REALITY

Thus we realize, illuminating and focusing the Eye of Faith is not a fleeting, intangible, ethereal moment in time, but rather the literal organization or creation of veritable units of spiritual matter, as "all spirit is matter" (D&C 131:8).

We also know that the form and function of all things, in both the mortal physical world and in the divine spiritual world, are determined by their respective infrastructures, including levels of brightness and degrees of clarity when the Eye of Faith is illuminated and focused.

Furthermore, we know that the immensity of all creation is filled with radiating energies of invisible matter and, depending upon the sources from which they radiate and our receptiveness to them, they may either harmonize, align or synchronize to our enlightenment, or weaken, distort, impede, even nullify to our detriment.

Inasmuch as spiritual matter is invisible to our mortal observation, an examination of the brain reveals only an electro-chemical network of neurons, dendrites and neurotransmitters sharing information via synaptic exchanges.

However, permeating and giving life to that complex array of cerebral tissue, even at the atomic nucleus level, is our individual eternal spirit. For this reason, and others known to the Lord, what is referred to as the mind or the initiation of thought remains a mystery to modern science. Neuroscientists are recognizing something in addition to the brain, something invisible and of a higher nature, wherein lies the capacity to initiate a conceptualization and originate a thought at will. This is not a mystery to those who understand the plan of salvation, for "it is clear that the mind of man rests in the eternal spirit," and that "man's intelligence is in his spirit and not in the natural or mortal body."[6]

In fact, divine radiance to us as mortal beings completely ignores and bypasses the mortal body and brain and is "revealed to our spirits precisely as though we had no bodies at all"[7]

During mortality we experience a complexity of emotions and react to and make decisions in a myriad of events and circumstances from which an increasing array of radiant ◯s and ⬤s form automatically and continually in a life-long process.

Our ◯s and ⬤s in the active domain, in a marvelous electro-chemical relationship between the divine spirit and the mortal brain, are able to tune in to or receive incoming radiance and emit outgoing radiance. However, ◯s are only able to receive from and transmit to ◯s that are mutually in phase or in harmony with the respective one in the active domain. In like manner, and unfortunately, the ⬤s will attract relevant ⬤s that are congruous or compatible with ⬤s already in the active domain.

Because each and every ◯ and ⬤ is striving to fulfill its intent or purpose by attracting congruous or compatible ones (whether good or bad) and repelling incongruous, incompatible or opposing ones (whether good or bad), the content of the active domain determines at any given moment what we perceive and thus what we believe, whether right or wrong.

We also know that those veritable units of matter are able to be, and will be, reviewed and evaluated well into the future, for they remain in "a perfect remembrance" (Alma 5:18), because even "our thoughts will also condemn us" (Alma 12:14).

We realize further that our ◯s including ⬤s in the active domain are electro-chemical forms of energy, oscillating at frequencies detectable to us both spiritually and mortally as life-like

---

[6] Bruce R. McConkie, *Mormon Doctrine*, p. 501.

[7] *Scriptural Teachings of the Prophet Joseph Smith*, p. 398.

images with accompanying sounds and feelings we perceive as reality.

However, as shown throughout this book, our perceptions, for a variety of reasons, may be complete distortions of what is and is not reality.

The realities and truths of the eternities are found only in their purity and entirety in the Gospel of Jesus Christ. "True doctrine, understood, changes attitudes and behavior," asserts President Boyd K. Packer. "The study of the doctrines of the gospel will improve behavior quicker than a study of behavior will improve behavior."[8]

In the words of President Ezra Taft Benson,

> The Lord works from the inside out. The world works from the outside in. The world would take people out of the slums. Christ takes the slums out of people, and then they take themselves out of the slums. The world would mold men by changing their environment. Christ changes men, who then change their environment. The world would shape human behavior, but Christ can change human nature."[9]

The more we read, listen to and occupy our minds with eternal truths and divine realities, the more we accumulate desirable ⬤s, and thus the more sensitive we become to the light of Christ, the more receptive we become to the Holy Ghost, and the more able we become to perceive and comprehend truth and reality. As our comprehension of truth increases, and our perception of reality becomes more accurate, our own personal spirit becomes more capable of controlling the mortal body, our behavior and our spirituality.

The gospel-centered Eye of Faith illuminants and the "Essential Foundation ✺"s in chapter 3, in harmony with our personal aspirations, all combine to help us bring those powerful radiating energies into harmony with the eternal truths of the Gospel of Jesus

---

[8] *Conference Report*, Oct. 1986. p. 20.
[9] *Born of God, The Teachings of Ezra Taft Benson*, p. 79.

Christ, detect adversarial deceptions and focus through worldly distortions to see "things as they really are, and . . . as they really will be" (Jacob 4:13).

Otherwise, we misinterpret, we misunderstand, we miscommunicate. In the necessary "opposition in all things" (2 Nephi 2:11) we lose perspective and "call evil good, and good evil" (2 Nephi 15:20). We fall prey to those "expert in the devices of the devil" (Alma 11:21). We may discover too late that the adversary has "exercised his power" in us (Alma 12:5). We will find ourselves among those "who are blinded by the subtle craftiness of men" (D&C 123:12). We will fail to see "things as they really are" and remain unable to see "things as they really will be" (Jacob 4:13).

The receptiveness of our ●s, therefore, determines our capacity to be enlightened by the Light of Christ and prompted by the Power of the Holy Ghost. Then, once we are prepared for and receive the Gift of the Holy Ghost, and live worthy of his constant companionship, our ●s may harmonize with eternal truths in a manner never before possible.

The key to this glorious and divine interaction is the content of the active domain: the ever accumulating ●s, including numerous reality-distorting, life-damaging, marriage-wrecking, relationship-shattering, chemical-dependency, improvement-blocking, heart-hardening and mind-blinding ●s.

Radiant and powerful ☀s are the only way to literally and everlastingly replace ●s by brightly illuminating and clearly focusing the Eye of Faith, thereby harmonizing our radiance with the divine radiant sources of all reality, all truth and light.

Although this book was written to enable and encourage you to illuminate and focus your Eye of Faith in the spiritual realm, it is important to realize also that our mortal physiology produces dramatic results in temporal pursuits and objectives.

In fact, although they do not understand what all is happening, some of the processes included in the Eye of Faith Illuminants are attracting the increased attention of researchers in the behavioral and medical sciences.

Eye of FAITH HOPE AND CHARITY

Hope is a companion to faith. Because some people find it difficult to distinguish between the two, the two terms are often used interchangeably. They are different, however, and the difference is important to understand. *Faith* is a state of mind. *Hope* is a feeling or an emotion.

Faith is an unquestioned, unconditional acceptance that requires no proof, a conscious decision, complete, unwavering trust.

Hope, on other hand, is a feeling, deeply felt, a wishful expectation that what we want will happen. In fact, it is at the hope stage that it is so very important to focus the Eye of Faith with as much clarity and brightness as possible:

> Wherefore, ye must press forward with a steadfastness in Christ, having a perfect brightness of hope, and a love of God and of all men. Wherefore, if ye shall press forward, feasting upon the word of Christ, and endure to the end, behold, thus saith the Father: Ye shall have eternal life (2 Nephi 31:20).

Hope, however, is not complete assurance. Hope leads to Faith and is essential to Faith. In fact, we cannot have Faith without Hope. Moroni quoted his father Mormon: "How is it that ye can attain unto faith, save ye shall have hope?" (Moroni 7:40)

Hopelessness is also a feeling or an emotion: one of doom. In this frame of mind we assume any effort will be useless, and we have no confidence in a favorable outcome. Hopelessness leads to despondency. We stop trying and we give up. Once we give up, we are in despair. This is one of the lowest frames of mind, often accompanied by unrighteous living. "And if ye have no hope ye must needs be in despair; and despair cometh because of iniquity" (Moroni 10:22).

The formula for moving from despair to hope, and from hope to faith, contains one more vital and essential ingredient: ". . . and if there must be faith, there must also be hope; and if there must be hope there must also be charity" (Moroni 10:20).

"Above all things," the Lord says, "clothe yourselves with the bond of charity, as with a mantle, which is the bond of perfectness and peace" (D&C 88:125). We are commanded to seek and attain charity (see D&C 121:45; 124:116; 2 Nephi 33:7-9; Alma 7:24) and, furthermore, we are not even to assist in the Lord's work without charity (see D&C 12:8; 18:19). In fact, we are told more than once that we are "nothing" without charity (2 Nephi 26:30; Moroni 7:44).

Notice the powerful ✸s upon which we may focus our Eye of Faith in the following description of charity:

> And charity suffereth long, and is kind, and envieth not, and is not puffed up, seeketh not her own, is not easily provoked, thinketh no evil, and rejoiceth not in iniquity but rejoiceth in the truth, beareth all things, believeth all things, hopeth all things, endureth all things" (Moroni 7:44-48).

It is important to recognize the manner in which the three attributes are inter-related. As Moroni explains:

> And except ye have charity ye can in nowise be saved in the kingdom of God; neither can ye be saved in the kingdom of God if ye have not faith; neither can ye if ye have no hope" (Moroni 10:21).

Then, as we acquire and develop these attributes, our good works will follow. "And see that ye have faith, hope, and charity, and then ye will always abound in good works" (Alma 7:24).

We thus place a marvelous cycling process in motion as each interdependent attribute enhances and strengthens the other in a continual upward spiral.

If we continue to strive earnestly to do what is right, in the face of opposition and disappointment, we keep a spark of hope alive, a spark from which we may focus our Eye of Faith upon the pos-

Illustration 37

sibilities for overcoming difficulties, upon the potentials in ourselves and loved ones, upon the opportunities to experience charity or "the pure love of Christ" (Moroni 7:47), and upon ways to uplift and serve others.

Eye of Faith IN ADVERSITY AND TRIAL

In this chapter, we have seen a glimpse of the marvelous power of the Eye of Faith. We must also understand, however, that for reasons known to the Lord, our faith must and will be tried. In the translated words of Moroni: "ye receive no witness until after the trial of your faith" (Ether 12:6).

The Book of Mormon is replete with examples of how righteousness leads to prosperity and then, as people become more and more prosperous, pride and eventually wickedness sets in, and they fall. If awakening and focusing the Eye of Faith always and immediately brought the desired blessing, it would actually be to our detriment. We would mistakenly begin to think the power is in ourselves and, almost without realizing it, we would be relying on the "arm of flesh." (2 Nephi 4:34; 28:31; Helaman 4:13; D&C 1:19) For these and other reasons we "must be tried in all things" (D&C 101:4-5; 136:31).

Each one of us will experience trials of our faith in ways that are unique to us. What might be a trial of faith for one person may not be an adequate test for another.

In the words of the Prophet Joseph Smith:

> You will have all kinds of trials to pass through. And it is quite as necessary that you be tried as it was for Abraham and other men of God and . . . God will feel after you, and he will take hold of you and wrench your very heart strings and if you cannot stand it you will not be fit for an inheritance in the Celestial Kingdom of God"[10]

Elder Neal A. Maxwell acknowledges the power of the Eye of Faith in his creative and stimulating manner to inspire those with hope: "True, those with genuine hope may see their proximate circumstances shaken like a kaleidoscope at times, yet with the eye of faith they still see divine design"[11]

In the heartening quote above, and in the following encouraging and inspiring statement by Elder Maxwell, notice how vivid and colorful the ⬤s become as you experience your Eye of Faith cutting through the ever-changing array of colors and designs to a clear view of divine purpose in your life: "Let the kaleidoscope of life's circumstances be shaken, again and again, and the 'true believer of Christ' will still see with the *eye of faith* divine design and purpose in his life"[12] (italics added).

Actually, in a glorious manner, our trials may become blessings if we are "faithful in tribulation . . . For after much tribulation come the blessings" (D&C 58:2-4), and if we are "patient in affliction" (D&C 31:9) and avoid complaining or "murmuring" (1 Nephi 3:6; 17:49; D&C 9:6), we will experience that choice process of purification and "sanctification" (Helaman 3:35).

---

[10] John Taylor, *Journal of Discourses,* vol. 24, p. 197.

[11] Conference Report, April, 2001, *Ensign,* May 2001).

[12] *The Neal A. Maxwell Quote Book,* p. 197, from *True Believers in Christ,* p. 139.

In the midst of adversity and trial, there is no more powerful way to remain steadfast and endure faithfully than to prayerfully awaken the Eye of Faith and clearly focus upon appropriate and relevant ☼s of eternal truths. By so doing, we are seeing "things as they really are" and . . .

Eye of Faith:
SEEING THINGS AS THEY REALLY WILL BE

Although we may say some things are true for only a moment or a day, or a year or so, truth in the sense "of things as they really are, and of things as they really will be" (Jacob 4:13), are realities or truths that are unchanging and eternal. The Lord revealed through the Prophet Joseph Smith that "truth abideth and hath no end" (D&C 88:66).

No more powerful way exists to truly see "things as they really will be" than to worthily awaken, brightly illuminate and clearly focus the Eye of Faith upon long-range ☼s of eternal perspective.

Because the pressures of daily life and the seemingly endless demands upon our time tend to blur our perspective, it is all the more important that we strive for an eternal perspective. As Elder Neal A Maxwell said, "Time can tug at us and play so many tricks upon us if we lack eternal perspective."[13]

"When we know that this earthly estate is but one station along the road to immortality and life," said President Gordon B. Hinckley, "things take on an entirely different perspective."[14]

Although we have no instrument capable of measuring perfect or ideal perception, it stands to reason that the closer our perception of reality approaches not only "things as they really are" but also "things as they really will be" (Jacob 4:13), the more accurate will be our perspective of truth, the more strength will we have to

---

[13] Neal A. Maxwell, *Things As They Really Are*, p. 29.

[14] Gordon B. Hinckley, Temple Presidents Seminar, August 15, 1989, in *Teachings of Gordon B. Hinckley*, p. 431.

endure trials well without murmuring, the more capacity will we have to organize our lives according to divine priorities and thereby wisely prepare for eternal life.

It is very important that the ⬤s in our active domains be tempered with a long-range view, an eternal perspective, in every aspect of our lives. Whether failure or success, affliction or well-being, disappointment or encouragement, sorrow or joy, defeat or victory, the eternal point of view will place each condition in proper perspective and help us approach every circumstance in the most appropriate manner.

As President James E. Faust asserts, "For some, the refiner's fire causes a loss of belief and faith in God, but those with eternal perspective understand that such refining is part of the perfection process."[15]

Living the Gospel will be much more natural for us if we view the commandments through the Eye of Faith and clearly see the eternal perspective, because "When his commandments teach us," the Prophet Joseph Smith said, "it is in view of eternity; for we are looked upon by God as though we were in eternity. God dwells in eternity, and does not view things as we do."[16]

With respect to our well-being, the importance of an eternal view is stressed by Elder Russell M. Nelson: "For relief of an ailment, as a doctor of medicine I might write a prescription. As an ordained Apostle, I would invoke the spiritual blessing of eternal perspective."[17]

In every realm of endeavor, we would do well to remember: "Time is numbered only to man," reminded President Ezra Taft Benson, "God has your eternal perspective in mind."[18]

---

[15] James E Faust, "The Refiner's Fire," *Ensign*, May 1979, p. 53.

[16] Joseph Smith, *Teachings of the Prophet Joseph Smith*, p. 356.

[17] Russell M. Nelson, *Perfection Pending, and Other Favorite Discourses*, p. 98.

[18] Ezra Taft Benson, *Come, Listen to a Prophet's Voice*, p. 58.)

What a blessing it would be if the myriad of ⬤s in every realm of our lives embraced an eternal perspective. As President Spencer W. Kimball said: "If we looked at mortality as the whole of existence, then pain, sorrow, failure, and short life would be calamity. But if we look upon life as an eternal thing stretching far into the pre-earth past and on into the eternal post-death future, then all happenings may be put in proper perspective."[19]

It becomes obvious that a very long-range view, indeed an eternal perspective, is not only desirable but is imperative. Knowing this, however, does not make it happen. In fact, in the face of our mortal earthly struggles, an eternal point of view is difficult to achieve, even if we agree that such a view is preferable. What then can we do to change the mortal view, a view that thrusts itself upon us so automatically?

The answer is: the incomparable Eye of Faith, the most powerful and everlasting way to replace a mortal short-term view with an eternal perspective so strongly recommended by latter-day apostles and prophets.

"And if your eye (it is clear here the Lord is not referring to our mortal eyes) be single to my glory, your whole bodies shall be filled with light, and there shall be no darkness in you; and that body which is filled with light comprehendeth all things" (D&C 88:67).

Of all the many things we are learning by examining the atom, exploring the depths of the sea and searching into the outer reaches of space, none approach the significance of what we may learn from ancient and latter-day revelation about ourselves: who we really are as divine eternal spirits clothed only temporarily in mortal bodies, and the supernal relationship between our eternal spirits and our mortal intellects that will determine so much of what our lives will be in the eternities to come.

---

[19] Spencer W. Kimball, quoted in Neal A. Maxwell, *All These Things Shall Give Thee Experience*, p. 42.

Revealed light and truth make it clear that when (1) the Eye of Faith is righteously awakened, brightly illuminated and clearly focused, and (2) the real you, your eternal spirit, initiates ✷s (3) in compliance with the laws upon which ✷s are predicated, to which (4) your mortal intellect responds (5) in the divine process presented herein . . . you (6) open channels through which divine communication flows, (7) see the eternal perspective, (8) come closer unto Christ, (9) disable adversarial influences, (10) see the potential in others more as He sees their potential, (11) feel genuine love for others more, as He feels genuine love for them, (12) discover joy in serving others as He rejoices in our service, (13) recognize problems and trials as opportunities and blessings, (14) become far more receptive to inspiration from and through the Holy Ghost, (15) advance from a mortal state of mind to a divine point of view, and (16) literally overcome the "natural man" to (17) achieve unwavering levels of faith and (18) attain any blessing that is expedient and of which Heavenly Father approves.

So . . .

whether in the hurried moment of an important decision . . .

or a calm and solemn plea

for a blessing in behalf of someone . . .

whether riddled with discouragement,

hardships and trials . . .

or rejoicing in and teaching the great plan of happiness . . .

whether comforting, uplifting, inspiring and serving . . .

or struggling toward a personal life-long quest . . .

. . . illuminate and focus your Eye of Faith!

BIBLIOGRAPHY

Benson, Ezra Taft, "Jesus Christ, Gifts and Expectations." *The New Era,* May 1975.

_____. "Born of God," *The Teachings of Ezra Taft Benson,* Salt Lake City, Utah, Bookcraft, 1988.

_____. "Think On Christ," *Ensign,* April, 1985.

_____. *Come, Listen to a Prophet's Voice,* Salt Lake City, Utah; Deseret Book Company, 1990.

_____. *The Teachings of Ezra Taft Benson,* Salt Lake City, Utah; 1994.

Faust, James E., "The Refiner's Fire," *Ensign,* May, 1979.

_____. First Presidency Message, "That We Might Know Thee," *Ensign,* January, 1999.

Hinckley, Gordon B., Temple Presidents Seminar, August 15, 1989, in *Teachings of Gordon B. Hinckley,* Salt Lake City, Utah; Deseret Book Company, 1997.

_____. Conference Report, October 14, 2000, *Ensign,* November, 2000.

Kimball, Spencer W., quoted in Neal A. Maxwell, *All These Things Shall Give Thee Experience,* Salt Lake City, Utah; Deseret Book Company, 1979.

_____. *The Miracle of Forgiveness,* Salt Lake City, Utah, Bookcraft, 1969.

Lee, Harold B., *Youth and the Church,* Salt Lake City, 1945.

Maxwell, Neal A., *A Time To Choose.*

_____. Conference Report, April, 2001, *Ensign,* May, 2001.

_____. *The Neal A. Maxwell Quote Book,* Salt Lake City, Utah; Bookcraft, 1997.

_____. *Things As They Really Are,* Salt Lake City, Utah; Deseret Book Company, 1978.

McConkie, Bruce R., *Mormon Doctrine,* 2d ed. Salt Lake City, Utah, Bookcraft,

McConkie, Joseph Fielding, *Gospel Symbolism,* Salt Lake City, Utah; Bookcraft.

McKay, David O., *Conference Report,* April, 1950.

_____. *Man May Know For Himself,* 1967.

Nelson, Russell M., from an address to Religious Educators, 13 Sept. 1985, published by the Church Educational System.

_____. *Perfection Pending, and Other Favorite Discourses,* Salt Lake City: Deseret Book Company, 1998.

Packer, Boyd K., "The Cloven Tongues of Fire," Conference Report, *Ensign,* May, 2000.

_____. "What Is Faith?" in *Faith.*

_____. *Teach Ye Diligently,* Salt Lake City, Utah; Deseret Book Company, 1975.

_____. *Conference Report,* October. 1986.

Smith, Joseph, *History of the Church,* (Edited by B. H. Roberts, Salt Lake City, Utah; Vol. 3, Vol. 5, Vol. 6.

_____. *Lectures on Faith,* Salt Lake City, Utah; Deseret Book Company, 1985.

_____. *Teaching of the Prophet Joseph Smith,* selected and arranged by Joseph Fielding Smith, Salt Lake City, Utah; Deseret Book Company, 1977.

Talmage, James E., *A Study of the Articles of Faith,* Salt Lake City, Utah, Deseret Book Company, 1955.

Taylor, John, in *Journal of Discourses,* vol. 24, 197.

Webster, Noah, *Webster's New World Dictionary of the American Language,* William Collins Publishers, 1979.

Young, Brigham, *The Discourses of Brigham Young.* Selected and arranged by John A. Widtsoe, Salt Lake City, Utah; Deseret Book Company, 1961.

_____. *Journal of Discourses,* Liverpool: F.D. and S.W. Richards, 1854, Vol. 1.

SCRIPTURES
BOOK OF MORMON

1 Nephi
14:7
3:6
17:49
17:49
3:6

2 Nephi
2:11
2:11
2:14
2:25
2:26
4:34
6:63
11:4
15:20
25:29
27:5
28:31
30:6
31:13
31:20
31:21
31:21
33:7-9

Jacob
4:13
4:14

Enos
1:27

Jarom
1:3

Mosiah
2:11
3:17
3:19
3:19

4:6
4:11
6:9
10:12

Alma
4:11
5:1
5:15
5:15
5:16
5:16
5: 17-18
5:18
5:18
5:48
7: 23-24
7:24
7:24
11:21
11:21
11:21
12:4
12:5
13:14
14:6
22:16
22:18
28:21
30:2-28
32: 40
32:42
32:17
32:27
32:27
32:27
32:28-42
32:28
32:40

32:42
33:1
33:22
33:23
39:13
41:11
42:8

Helaman
3:35
4:13

3 Nephi
13:22
13:23
17:3
13:24
17:7
27:27
7:16

Ether
4:12
15:19 (5+)

Moroni
6:8
7:26
7:33
7:40
7:44-48
7:47
7:6
7:9
7:16-18
10:4
10:4
10:20
10:21
10:22
10:23
10:32

DOCTRINE AND COVENANTS

Explanatory	31:9	88:67
Introduction	31:12	88:67
1:19	32:4	88:126
4:2	33:17	89:4
5:24	50:24	90:
6:38	58:2	93:2
6:38	58:2-4	93:49
9:11	58:26-28	98:47
9:3	58:9	100: 6
9:6	59:5	101:16
9:6	61:39	101:4-5
10:5	75:11	101:7
10:70; 45:7; 50:24,27	81:3	101:8
12:8	84:45	105:19
12:9	84:46	121:45
14:8	84:85	123:12
18:18	84:85	124:1162
18:18	88:7-13	130:20-21
18:19	88:125	130:21
19:38	88:64	131:7-8
20:33	88:66	132:22
29:34	88:67	136:31
31:9		

PEARL OF GREAT PRICE

Moses 6:52   Moses 6:63

NEW TESTAMENT

Matthew
6:22
14:22-32

Luke
10:27

Mark
12:30

Galatians
6:7

1 Corinthians
2:14

OLD TESTAMENT

Genesis
1:11-12, 27-28

JST Genesis
6:53

Ezekiel
12:2

INDEX

A

Active Domain–32-36, 41, 58, 78, 80, 83, 85, 87, 89 , 90, 92, 104, 108, 132, 134, 137, 140-141, 143-144, 146, 148, 150
Addictions–15, 59, 79, 92-93, 101-103, 111, 119, 121
Adversity–153-155
Aesthetic Realm–116
Affectionate Realm–116
Affliction–62, 72, 73,97, 98, 154, 156
Agency–2, 16, 36, 37, 40, 48, 86, 87,116, 118, 145
Alma
    On Casting About Eyes–19
    On Awake, Arouse Faculties–19, 25
    On Giving A Place–19
    On Likening Word to Seed–19, 20, 22, 81, 127
Anxiety–29, 50, 56, 99, 111, 113,
Apple–30
Arm of Flesh–88, 117, 153
Atomic Nucleus–43, 147
Atonement–56, 63, 74, 117, 136
Attitude–18, 33, 83, 95, 118, 126, 149,
Attracting Power–143, 145, 148
Attributes To Recognize–89, 91, 93, 105, 119, 126
Autonomic Nervous System–28, 36, 37

B

Behavior–16, 27, 37, 58, 75, 80, 84, 85, 88, 90, 94, 102, 105, 109, 135, 140, 149,
Belief Believe Believing–2, 17, 18, 19, 20,23, 26, 27, 31, 33, 34, 36, 50, 64, 68, 70, 72, 73, 85, 87, 88, 91, 94, 99, 101, 105, 106, 109, 111, 123, 126, 127, 130, 148, 152, 156
Benson, Ezra Taft
    On Taking Time to Ponder–46
    On What Would Jesus Do?–61
    On Turning Life Over To God–99, 100
    On Lord Works From Inside Out–149

Blessings to Pronounce–59, 75, 115, 119
Blindness Of Mind–20, 22, 25, 106, 108,
Brain
    Damage Of–77, 81, 82
    Hemispheric Differences–110, 111, 128
    Relationship to Spirit–25, 27, 37-40, 43, 44, 50, 56, 59, 75, 81, 87, 109, 110, 111, 123, 128, 129, 148
    Waves–112, 113

C

Callings to Magnify–119
Challenges–79, 119
Charity–65, 107, 151, 152, 153
Child of God–65, 89, 105
Children to Guide–90, 93-95, 119
Colorblind–14
Color Spectrum–82, 142
Commanding Spiritually–38, 43, 44, 47, 56, 83, 89, 113, 118, 123, 135
Communication (See *Divine Communication*)
Confidences To Build–93-95, 119, 120, 127
Convictions–126
Corpus Callosum–129
Counseling–103-108

D

Darkness–104, 106, 157
Decisions–61, 107, 117, 119, 148
Decoding System–35, 36
Depression–77. 111
Despair–104, 119, 130, 151, 152
Devil, Devices Of–31, 78, 150
Disappointment–60, 79, 96, 97, 152, 156
Discouragement–79, 80, 96-98, 131, 158
Distorted Perception
Divine Communication–38, 44, 71, 102, 113, 130, 131, 134, 145, 158
Diving–119-120

E

Effectors–35-37
Eiffel Tower–20
Electromagnetic Energy–141-142
Emotions–28, 36, 49, 56, 111, 126, 148
Encoding System–36
Essential Foundations–60
Eternal Perspective–85, 88, 108, 109, 155-158

F

Facial Expressions–88, 90-92
Faith/Hope/Charity Cycle–152-153
Faust, James E.
   On How to Think of Heavenly Father During Prayer–51, 60
Fears–15, 29, 53, 56, 59, 60, 72, 94, 99, 113, 119, 125, 131, 132, 140
Frustration–96, 113, 130

G

Gestures–36, 88
Goals–112, 116, 117, 119, 121
God. (*See Heavenly Father; Jesus Christ*)
Grades–15, 116, 123
Grapefruit–31
Gratitude–57, 59, 64, 122, 123, 131, 135
Great Plan of Happiness–63, 66, 158

H

Habits–92, 102, 119, 129
Happiness–63, 66, 79, 89, 122, 123, 146, 158
Heart–19, 21, 26, 27, 28, 31, 43, 49, 54, 55, 64, 72, 94, 102, 102, 106, 131, 132, 150, 154
Heavenly Father–48, 49, 51, 53, 54-56, 59, 50, 62, 65-67, 96, 97, 104, 118, 131, 137, 158
Holy Ghost–16, 39, 46, 53-55, 60, 83, 85, 102, 103, 107, 115, 118, 132, 133-135, 137-140, 143, 149, 150, 158
Hope–19, 20, 33, 34, 36, 48, 59, 60, 77, 80, 82, 94-97, 99, 102, 104, 107, 126, 134, 146, 151, 152, 154
Hugging–90

I

Idle Spirit–83
Illuminants–48-57
Images–18, 132, 141
Inactive Domain–32, 35, 58, 80
Inception–82, 132, 141
Inconsequential Domain–33, 103
Infrastructures–140, 141, 147
Inspiration (See also *Divine Communication*)– 16, 38, 44, 49, 60, 78, 88, 103, 107, 115, 133, 158
Intelligences–44
Intra-dependence–117-118
Investigators–101-103, 123
Involuntary-autonomic Level–36

J

Jalopy Convertible–121-122
Jellybeans–13, 14, 144, 146, 147
Jesus Christ–20, 48, 61, 62, 65-67, 70, 72, 100, 149

K

Kimball, Spencer W.
   On Thoughts Being Recorded by Means Known Only to
     Higher Beings–30
   On Eternal Perspective–157

L

Lamanites–31
Law of Harvest–22
Laws–22, 27, 39, 48, 74, 88, 102, 123, 134, 137, 158
Learning–37, 39, 49, 55, 65, 110, 128, 129
Lee, Harold B.
   What Would He Do?–61
Lessons to Prepare–119
Light of Christ–104, 136, 137, 143, 149, 150
Light-sensitive Cells–145
London Temple–86
Love–21, 26, 56, 60, 65, 68, 70, 73, 74, 88, 89, 95, 100, 105, 115, 116, 122, 151, 153, 158

M

Marriage–15, 78, 89, 93, 119, 126, 150, 165,
Matter–135M 136M 140, 141, 147
Mcconkie, Bruce R.
    On Mind, Intelligence Is in Spirit, Not Mortal Body–148
Mckay, David O.
    On Light And Darkness in Mind–86
    On Personal Radiance–92, 145, 146
Mental Exertion–42, 47, 59, 67
Micromomentary Expressions–90, 91, 93, 94, 125, 126
Mind–30, 31, 37-39, 45, 46, 48, 49, 56, 66-74, 78, 79, 83, 88, 96, 99, 102, 112, 113
Misperception–33, 81, 90, 109
Missionary Work–101, 103, 123, 133, 139, 140
Motor Neurons–37, 91
Mustard Seed–22, 81

N

Natural Eye–19, 22, 25, 100, 106
Natural Man–41, 44, 55, 56, 75, 85, 86, 117, 135, 158
Nelson, Russel M.
    On Medical Knowledge and Priesthood Power–26
    On Eternal Perspective–156
Nephites–100

O

Opposition–77, 150, 152

P

Packer, Boyd K.
    On Believing Is Seeing–18
    On Improving Behavior–149
Paris–20
Perception–15, 28, 33, 81-83, 86-88, 90, 91, 109
Perceptual Screen–33-35, 41, 58, 83, 84, 104
Perfect Remembrance–29, 30, 56, 141, 148
Personal Radiance–92, 125, 145
Personality–80, 93
Phobias–15, 103
Photoreceptors–145

Physical Force–42, 47, 59
Plan of Salvation–38, 66, 148
Pomme–30-31, 132
Pomplemousse–31, 132
Ponder–45-46
Potential–16, 39, 65, 77, 89, 91, 93, 94, 101, 105, 108, 126, 153, 158
Prayer–45, 48-50, 53, 57, 60, 64, 75, 77, 83, 96, 102, 103, 106, 107, 115, 121, 122, 130-132, 135, 155
Promptings (See also *Divine Communication*)–*26, 46, 83, 107,* 113, 135, 137, 138
Pupillometric Research–91

R

Radiance Of Reality–135-136
Reality–28-30, 33, 50, 63, 74, 78, 81, 82, 85, 86, 92, 108, 109, 149, 150, 155
Receptors–35-37, 81, 84
Relationships–15, 29, 56, 74, 89, 90, 116, 119, 126, 165
Remembering–128
Repelling Power–143, 145, 148
Repentance–30, 54, 102
Respiratory System–28, 37
Revelation (See also *Divine Communication*)–23, 25, 39, 43, 44, 49, 74, 117, 133-135, 157

S

Scriptures–16, 22, 23, 33, 43, 47, 59, 77, 83, 111
Self-concept–80, 88
Smith, Joseph Jr.
    On Synonymity Of Mind, Spirit, Intelligence–38.
    On Divine Communication as Though No Body–133. 134, 138, 148
    Need to Stretch, Search, Contemplate–45
    On Mental Exertion–47, 59
    On Attributes of God–73
    On Trials for Inheritance–154
Smoking–102, 111
Somatic Nervous System–37
Speaking–15, 132, 33

Spirit-brain Relationship (See *Brain*)
Spiritual Power–89, 116, 132, 135
Spiritual Processing–43, 46
Spiritual Realm–115
Spirituality–80, 84, 89, 149
Standards to Uphold–119
Stimulus-response–22, 55
Sympathetic Nervous System–37
Synaptic Exchanges–32, 43, 147

T

Talks To Deliver–15, 119, 132, 133,
Talmage, James E.
   On Faith as Vivified, Vitalized Belief–18
Teenagers to Discipline–15, 75, 89, 90, 92, 93, 95, 108, 119
Temporal Power–27, 116, 118, 119-125
Temptations to Overcome–119
Test Taking–123-125
Testimonies To Strengthen–119
Therapeutic Realm–115
Tithing–74, 101
Transgression–57, 77, 85
Trespasses to Forgive–119
Trials and Tribulation–53, 72, 73, 79, 95, 97, 119, 153-156, 158
Triumphant Realm–116

U

Ultimate Command Level (See *Commanding Spiritually*)–38
Uplifting Others–92, 125, 153, 158

V

Values–33, 126, 127
Vineyard–22
Vocal Inflection–36, 91
Voluntary-responsive Level–37

W

Wallet–96-97
Weaknesses to Replace–119
Well-being Realm–116
Wishful Thinking–47, 50, 56, 94, 126, 135,

Word of Wisdom–74, 78, 101-103, 121, 123, 139
Worry–29, 56, 62, 99

Y

Young, Brigham
    On Body Over Spirit–40
    On Greatest Lesson To Learn: Cannot Understanding Things Of God Without Learning Of Ourselves–39
    On Greatest Mystery To Know How To Control Human Mind–48

Z

Zarahemla–16, 57
Zeezrom–78

ABOUT THE AUTHOR

Ron L. McIntyre received his bachelor's and master's degrees from Brigham Young University and his Ph.D. from the Ohio State University. He has been a chief executive in public broadcasting and administered from top management levels in both radio and television.

A strong critic of television's impact upon society, Dr. McIntyre has been influential in the development of innovative and useful roles for the television medium and other modes of telecommunication and interpersonal relationships.

He has taught and designed new courses of study for four universities and is a marriage and family communication consultant.

He served as a missionary in the French-speaking areas of Belgium, Switzerland and France in what was then the French Mission. He has served in a variety of ward and stake leadership callings, as an Ordinance Worker in the Arizona Temple, and is now serving as an ordained Patriarch.

The author and his wife, Laurie Anne Burke McIntyre, have three daughters, nine grandchildren and reside in Mesa, Arizona.